Complete Web Applications using PHP and MySQL

With HTML5, CSS3 and JavaScript: Build a school Library Management System

By Rumaysa Ahmed

Complete Web Applications using PHP and MySQL

With HTML5, CSS3 and JavaScript: Build a school Library Management System

By Rumaysa Ahmed

February 2020: First edition

978-0-244-85829-2

Contents

INTRODUCTION

Welcome to Complete Web Applications using **PHP** and **MySQL**! This book will guide you through creating a web application: A Library Management System (LMS) for your school. A project that can also help you learn new PHP, CSS and HTML skills.

This book is aimed at anyone interested in learning and creating web applications using PHP, CSS3, JavaScript, HTML5 and MySQL. I am nine years old, love coding and creating web applications. I would like to see all children like me to be able to code and create their own web applications. Together, we can all be prepared for the future of computing technology.

NOTE:

- Children require a parent or guardian to help them register for the account that will be needed to set up and complete the project on the live web hosting.

- A parent or guardian should supervise children when using the internet.

You can check out the demo and get the source code from my website at: https://creativeproggrammer.atwebpages.com/.

To learn more about PHP, CSS and HTML, check out this website: https://www.w3schools.com/.

What are you waiting for?

Then let's get started!

Chapter 1: Setting up

Host our LMS

We are going to host our LMS on a live server. To do this, go to https://freewebhostingstudio.com/ and select free signup as shown below in Figure 1-1.

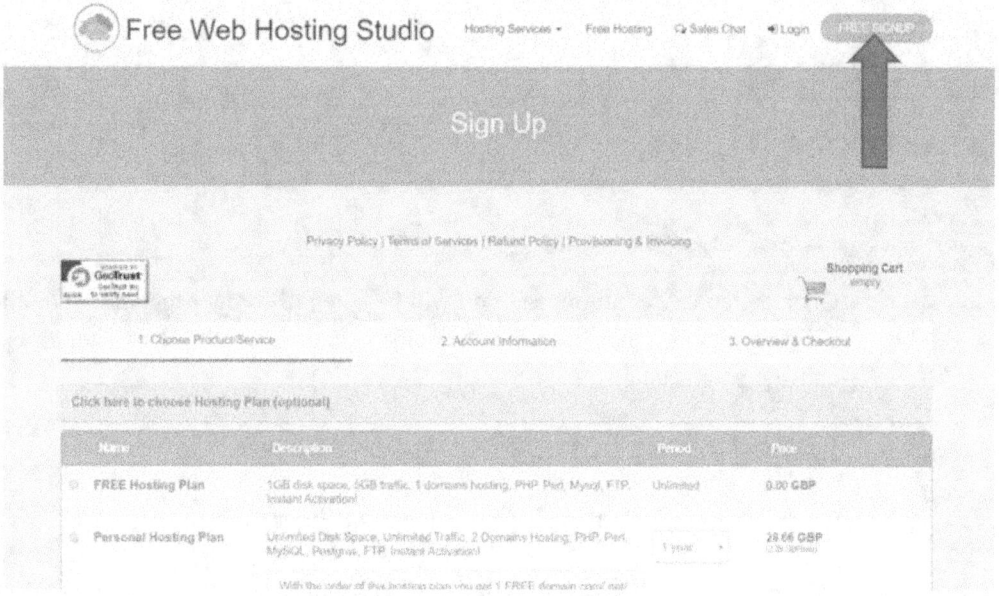

Figure 1-1: The signup page

Select the free hosting plan or, if you like, you can buy personal or business hosting plan. Also, you can buy a domain or transfer an existing domain. If you select free hosting plan, you get free hosting and free subdomains for your project. Then click 'Continue'. On the next page, you will need to include your details into the required fields as shown in Figure 1-2.

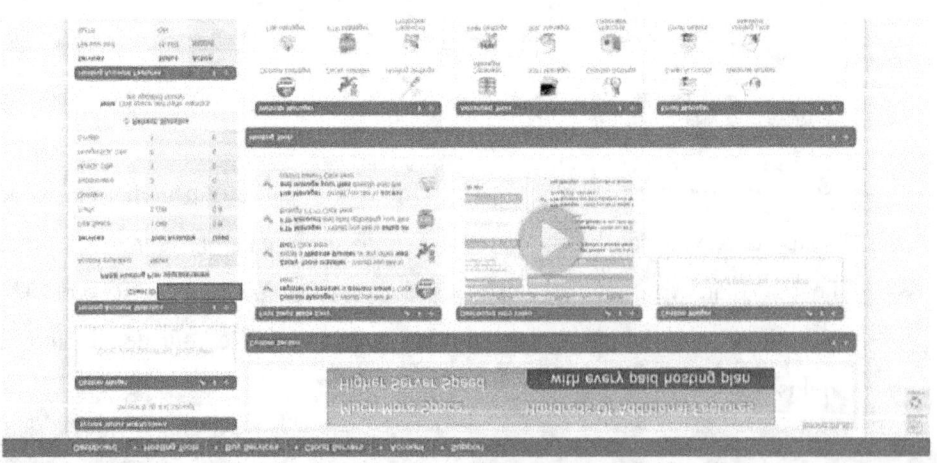

New Client

If you already have an account with us click ⬤ .

* required fields
* optional fields

* First Name:

* Last Name:

* Company:

* E-mail (provide valid e-mail):

* Password:

* Address 1:

* City: * State: * ZIP:

* Country:
United Kingdom

* Phone:

☐ Yes, I agree with the following agreement(s): Terms of Services - FREE Hosting, Refund Policy and Privacy Policy.

☐ I'm not a robot

CONTINUE »

Figure 1-2: The signup page; enter your details

Click the continue button, and you will be taken to a new page with your client ID and a link to login. Click the link to login to your account. Now check your email to activate your account.

Login to your hosting account

Once logged in, your homepage will look like Figure 1-3.

Figure 1-3: Your homepage

Create a domain or subdomain

Now we need to create a domain or subdomain name. Click the Domain Manager link, as shown in Figure 1-4.

Figure 1-4: Where you find your domain manager

You can now register a new domain or subdomain name; it can be whatever you like!

Create a database

Now we need to create a database that we will need for our LMS. I recommend you call it library.

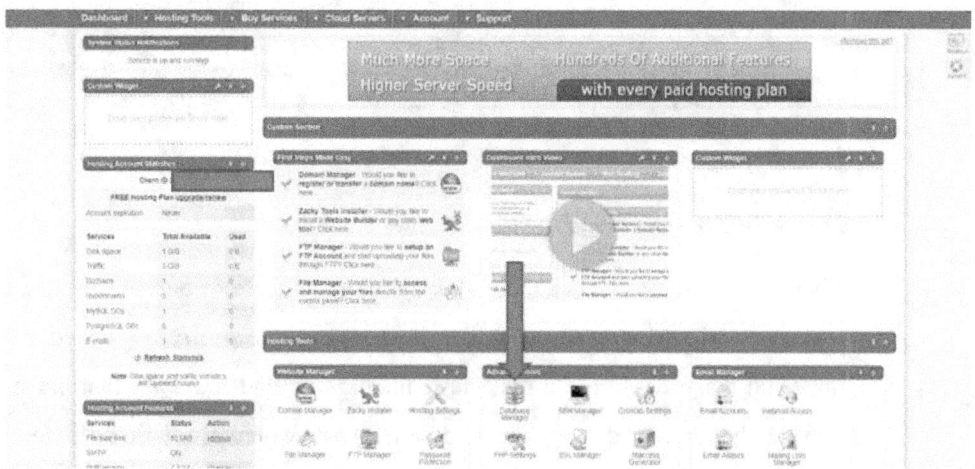

Figure 1-5: Where to create the database

Create your database by filling in the form in Figure 1-6.

| Database | Section Information | FAQ |

Create MySQL Database

Create PostgreSQL
Database

Create MySQL Database

Database Name	3203090_name
Database Password	(8-32 alphanumeric chars)
	Please provide a password.
Confirm Database Password	(8-32 alphanumeric chars)
Database Version	5.7

Create Database

Figure 1-6: The database form

Creating directories

Finally, we are going to setup our file manager.

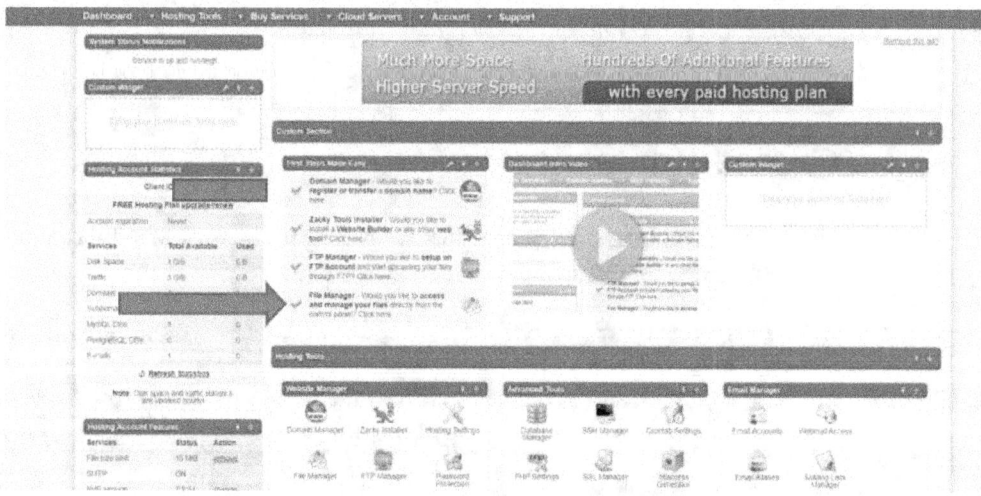

Figure 1-7: Where to find the file manager

There should be one folder there already with the name of our domain name. Click on it and you will have an empty folder. Now create a new directory called *library*. Click on it and make two more directories called *admin* and *student*. Then make a new file outside the *library* directory called ***index.php***, where we will be able to navigate between the *admin* and *student* pages.

5

Chapter 2: Working on our database

Going back to our database manager, we are now going to click on the link to take us to phpMyAdmin.

Creating an admin table

First, create a table called admin. We will store the admin's data here and you will need to enter the requested information as shown in Figure 2-1.

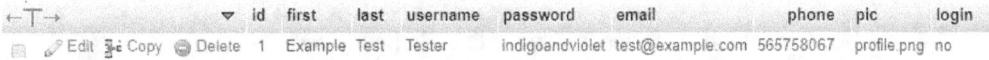

	id	first	last	username	password	email	phone	pic	login
Edit ⅜ Copy ⊜ Delete	1	Example	Test	Tester	indigoandviolet	test@example.com	565758067	profile.png	no

Figure 2-1: The columns in our admin table

Creating a student table

Now we need to make a table called student. We will store the student's data here. We will have the same columns. Figure 2-2 shows you how.

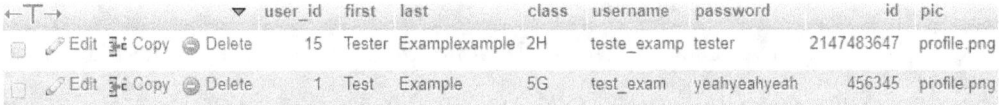

	user_id	first	last	class	username	password	id	pic
Edit ⅜ Copy ⊜ Delete	15	Tester	Examplexample	2H	teste_examp	tester	2147483647	profile.png
Edit ⅜ Copy ⊜ Delete	1	Test	Example	5G	test_exam	yeahyeahyeah	456345	profile.png

Figure 2-2: The columns in the student table

Creating a books table

Next make a table called books. We will store the books here. You can add the books mentioned below through the insert link and complete the columns as shown in Figure 2-3.

	bid	isbn	title	authors	publisher	status	quantity	section	description	image
Edit ⅜ Copy ⊜ Delete	1	9781652770459	Complete Web Applications using PHP and MySQL			Available	1	Computers/Web/Non-Fiction	Build a Library Management System for your school.	

Figure 2-3: The columns and books in our books table

Creating an issue_book table

Finally, we will need a table called issue_book. We will store the student's borrowed books here. Figure 2-4 shows you what columns are needed.

←T→	▽	ii_id	username	bid	approve	borrow_date	return_date
☐ ⬡ Edit ⬡ Copy ⬡ Delete		1	test_exam	1	Borrowed	2020-01-02	2020-02-06

Figure 2-4: Our issue_book columns

Connecting to the database

Now, we need to make our connection file to connect to the database. In your *admin* and *student* directories, make a file called ***connection.php***.

Figure 2-5 shows you how to code it.

```
<?php
    $db=mysqli_connect('                                                      ');
    /* server name, username, password, database name */
?>
```

Figure 2-5: Our connection file

The server name will be ***fdb21.runhosting.com*** if you are using the free hosting plan and ***pdb21.runhosting.com*** if you are using the paid hosting plan.

> **NOTE**: The username and database name will be the same and there will always be your client ID and an underscore before the name of the database.

When you need to connect to the database, you call it by including it in your files. You will see how to do this in the following chapters.

Chapter 3: Creating project files

Creating index.php

Get the cheat sheet from http://creativeproggrammer.atwebpages.com/source.php.

We are now going to create the project files. But in this chapter, we are only going to code the *index.php* file (that is outside of our *library* directory). We want *index.php* to look like Figure 3-1, which is the same as our landing page.

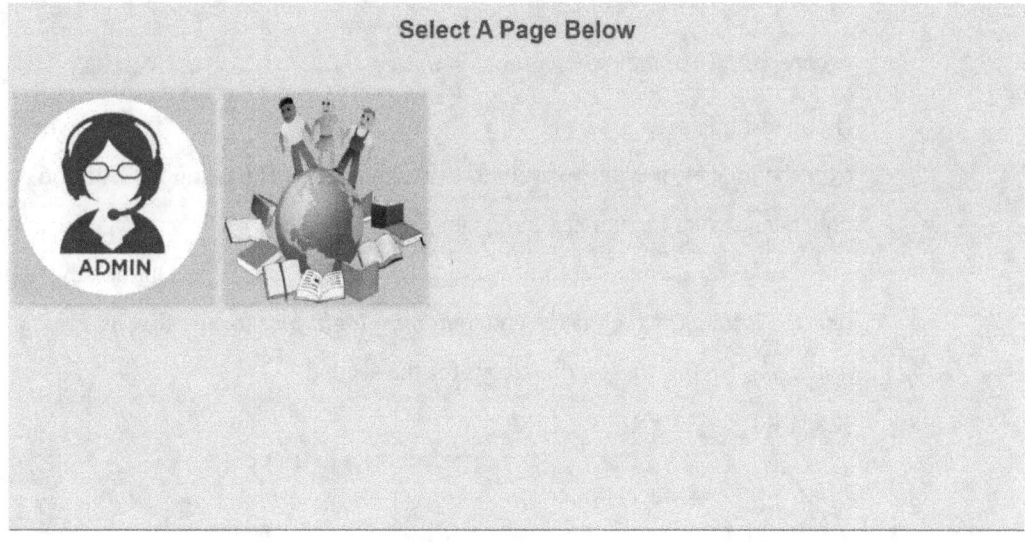

Figure 3-1: How we want index.php to look like

Before you look at the code, work out how to code this website using basic HTML knowledge. Figure 3-2 and Figure 3-3 show you what is on the other side of the images under the heading.

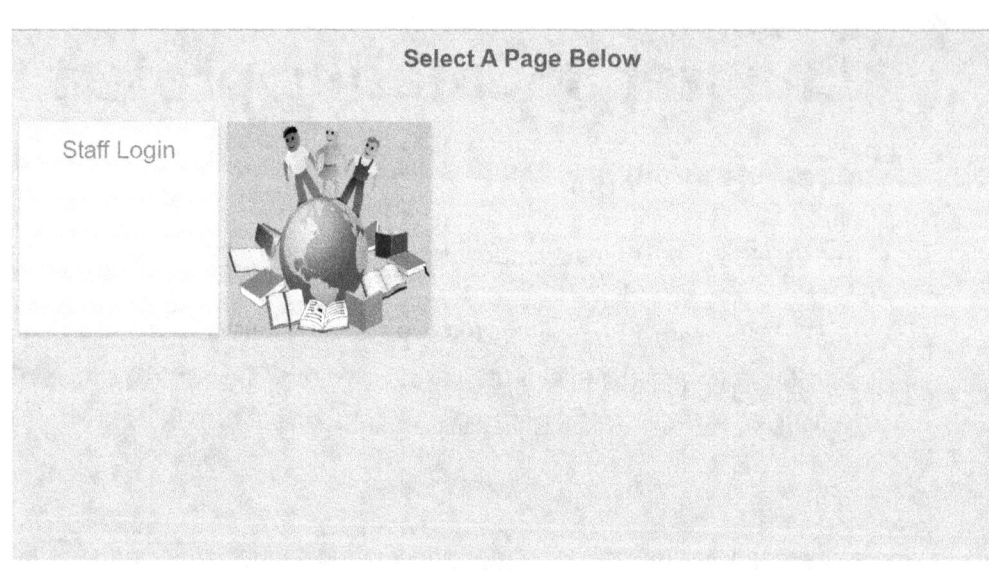

Figure 3-2: The other side of the first image

If you test this at http://creativeproggrammer.atwebpages.com/library/, when you hover over the images, it will flip around. You can make it flip using CSS. If you do not understand what I mean here, you can find out more at: https://www.w3schools.com/howto/howto_css_flip_card.asp. On the other side of the images, is a link, which takes you to *admin_login.php* for the first image and *index.php* (in the *student* directory) for the second.

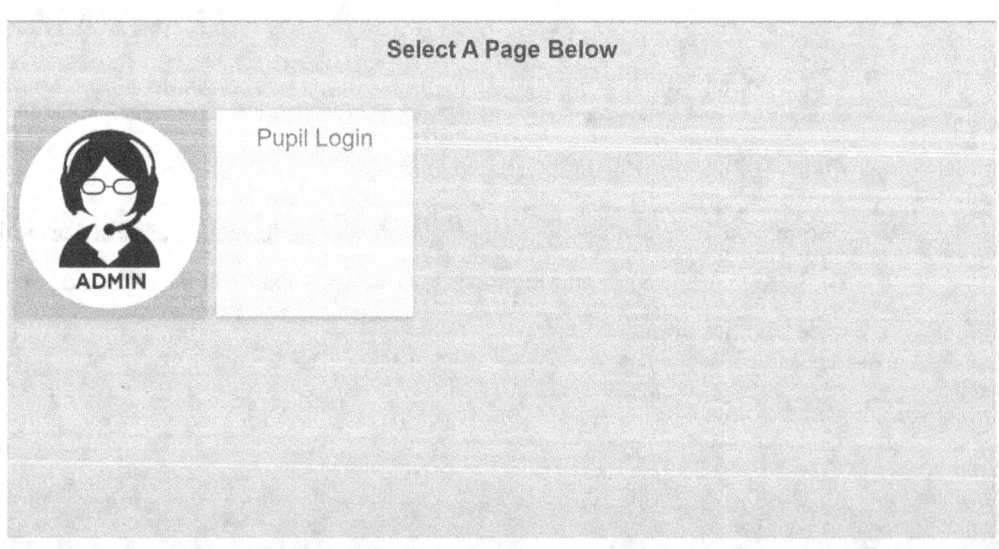

Figure 3-3: The other side of the second image

Coding index.php

Now let us have a look at the code. Figures 3-4 to 3-9 show you the code for *index.php*.

```
1  <!DOCTYPE HTML>
2  <html>
3      <head>
4          <title>Select A Page Below</title>
5          <meta name="viewport" content="width=device-width, initial-scale=1.0">
6          <style>
7              body
8              {
9                  background-color: lightgreen;
10                 color: blue;
11                 text-decoration: none;
12                 font-weight: bold;
13             }
14
15             * {box-sizing: border-box;}
16  body {font-family: Verdana, sans-serif;}
17  .mySlides {display: none;}
18  img {vertical-align: middle;}
19
20  /* Slideshow container */
21  .slideshow-container {
22    max-width: 1000px;
23    position: relative;
24    margin: auto;
25  }
26
27  /* Caption text */
28  .text {
29    color: #f2f2f2;
30    font-size: 15px;
31    padding: 8px 12px;
32    position: absolute;
33    bottom: 8px;
34    width: 100%;
35    text-align: center;
36  }
37
38  /* Number text (1/3 etc) */
39  .numbertext {
40    color: #f2f2f2;
```

Figure 3-4: The first part of index.php

In the first part, we declare our HTML document and open the **head** element. To find out more about declaring files and what the **head** tag is for, you can go to the following sites:

- https://www.w3schools.com/html/html_basic.asp and

- https://www.w3schools.com/tags/tag_head.asp

In the **head** element, give the page a title. It does not have to be Select A Page Below, it can be whatever you like! Then add a **meta** tag. The **meta** tag does not have a closing tag. For more information about using the **meta** tag, check this site: https://www.w3schools.com/tags/tag_meta.asp.

The parameters in the **content** attribute is to make the page responsive. Then open a **style** tag. The styling in the **style** tag are shown in Figures 3-4 to 3-6.

```
41    font-size: 12px;
42    padding: 8px 12px;
43    position: absolute;
44    top: 0;
45  }
46
47  /* The dots/bullets/indicators */
48  .dot {
49    height: 15px;
50    width: 15px;
51    margin: 0 2px;
52    background-color: #bbb;
53    border-radius: 50%;
54    display: inline-block;
55    transition: background-color 0.6s ease;
56  }
57
58  .active {
59    background-color: #717171;
60  }
61
62  /* Fading animation */
63  .fade {
64    -webkit-animation-name: fade;
65    -webkit-animation-duration: 5s;
66    animation-name: fade;
67    animation-duration: 5s;
68  }
69
70  @-webkit-keyframes fade {
71    from {opacity: .4}
72    to {opacity: 1}
73  }
74
75  @keyframes fade {
76    from {opacity: .4}
77    to {opacity: 1}
78  }
79
80  /* On smaller screens, increase text size */
```

Figure 3-5: Lines 41-80

```
81  @media only screen and (min-width: 300px) {
82    h1, h2 {font-size: 30px}
83  }
84
85  .flip-card {
86    background-color: transparent;
87    width: 300px;
88    height: 300px;
89    perspective: 1000px;
90  }
91
92  .flip-card-inner {
93    position: relative;
94    width: 100%;
95    height: 100%;
96    text-align: center;
97    transition: transform 0.6s;
98    transform-style: preserve-3d;
99    box-shadow: 0 4px 8px 0 rgba(0,0,0,0.2);
100 }
101
102 .flip-card:hover .flip-card-inner {
103   transform: rotateY(180deg);
104 }
105
106 .flip-card-front, .flip-card-back {
107   position: absolute;
108   width: 100%;
109   height: 100%;
110   backface-visibility: hidden;
111 }
112
113 .flip-card-front {
114   background-color: #bbb;
115   color: black;
116 }
117
118 .flip-card-back {
119   background-color: yellow;
120   color: white;
```

Figure 3-6: The third part of index.php

```
121     transform: rotateY(180deg);
122  }
123
124  a {
125      color: navy;
126      text-decoration: none;
127  }
128
129  a:hover {
130      color: red;
131      text-decoration: none;
132  }
133
134          </style>
135  <link rel="stylesheet" href="https://maxcdn.bootstrapcdn.com/bootstrap/3.4.0/css/bootstrap.min.css">
136  <script src="https://ajax.googleapis.com/ajax/libs/jquery/3.4.0/jquery.min.js"></script>
137  <script src="https://maxcdn.bootstrapcdn.com/bootstrap/3.4.0/js/bootstrap.min.js"></script>
138          </head>
139      <body style="background-color: lightgreen; color: blue;">
140          <h1 style="text-align: center;"><b>Select A Page Below</b></h1>
141          <div class="box" style="">
142          <div class="flip-card" style="position: relative; left: 10px;">
143      <div class="flip-card-inner">
144          <div class="flip-card-front">
145          <img src="https://www.logolynx.com/images/logolynx/23/23938578fb8d88c02bc59906d12230f3.png" alt="Avatar" style="width:300px;height:300p
146          </div>
147          <div class="flip-card-back">
148          <h1><a href="admin/admin_login.php">Staff Login</a></h1>
149          </div>
150          </div>
151  </div>
152  <br><br><br>
153  <div class="flip-card" style="position: relative; top: -360px; left: 325px;">
154      <div class="flip-card-inner">
155          <div class="flip-card-front">
156          <img src="https://upload.wikimedia.org/wikipedia/commons/thumb/c/c4/One_world_many_stories.svg/581px-One_world_many_stories.svg.png" al
157          </div>
158          <div class="flip-card-back">
159          <h1><a href="student/index.php">Pupil Login</a></h1>
160          </div>
```

Figure 3-7: Lines 121-160

Once you have completed the styling, add links to Bootstrap. To get the links, you can go to https://www.w3schools.com/bootstrap/default.asp. Close the **head** element. Open the **body** element. Add a **style** attribute and make the **background-color** light green (or a colour of your choice) and the **color** blue (or whatever you like!). Inside the **body** element, open a **h1** element and get a **style** attribute. In the **style** attribute, **text-align** should be set to center. Then open a **b** element and type whatever you typed in the **title** tag. In my case, I entered Select A Page Below in my title **tag** so that is what goes in the **h1** tag. Underneath it, open a **div** element and give it the **class** box. Inside the **div** element, open another **div** element and assign it to the **class** flip-card (or you can cheat and copy the code from here: https://www.w3schools.com/howto/howto_css_flip_card.asp).

Get the **style** attribute. Inside the **style** attribute, add the CSS properties **position** and **left**. **Position** should be set to relative and **left** 10px. Then open another **div** element and assign it to the **class** flip-card-inner. Put another **div** tag and assign it to the **class** flip-card-front. Get an **img** tag. You can set the **src** attribute to any image you like and the **alt** attribute to anything you like. Want to find out more about the **img** tag? Check out this site: https://www.w3schools.com/tags/tag_img.asp.

12

Add a **style** attribute and inside it there should be width set to 300px and height also set to 300px. Close the **div** tag and open a new **div** element. Assign it to the **class** flip-card-back. Inside this tag, open a **h1** tag and open the **a** tag. The href attribute will be *admin/admin_login.php*. The text will be Staff Login. Close the remaining **div** tags and add three **br** tags.

Repeat the process of making the **div** tag assigned to the **class** flip-card. The only difference is, in the first **div** tag that you open, left will be set to 325px and add a top which is set to -360px. In the **a** tag, change the href attribute from *admin/admin_login.php* to *student/index.php*.

```
161     </div>
162  </div>
163        </div>
164      <center>
165      <div class="slideshow-container" style="">
166
167         <h1>Books of the Week</h1><br>
168
169  <div class="mySlides fade">
170     <img src="https://images-na.ssl-images-amazon.com/images/I/51WuLKfJktL._SX324_BO1,204,203,200_.jpg" style="width: 200px; height: 200px;"
171     <br><br><br><br>
172     <div class="text" style="color: blue;">Showtime, Jean Ure, 3 May 2018</div>
173  </div>
174
175  <div class="mySlides fade">
176     <img src="https://images-na.ssl-images-amazon.com/images/I/51%2BV5g3Q9WL._SX324_BO1,204,203,200_.jpg" style="width: 200px; height: 200px
177     <br><br><br><br>
178     <div class="text" style="color: blue;">Catching Falling Stars, Karen McCombie,  4 June 2015</div>
179  </div>
180
181  <div class="mySlides fade">
182     <img src="https://images-na.ssl-images-amazon.com/images/I/C1JITGIwOGL.jpg" style="width: 200px; height: 200px;">
183     <br><br><br>
184     <div class="text" style="color: blue;">The Pearl in the Attic, Karen McCombie, June 2017</div>
185  </div>
186
187  </div>
188  <br>
189
190  <div style="text-align:center">
191     <span class="dot"></span>
192     <span class="dot"></span>
193     <span class="dot"></span>
194  </div>
195  </center>
196
197  <script>
198  var slideIndex = 0;
199  showSlides();
200
```

Figure 3-8: The fifth part of index.php

Add a **center** tag. Now open a new **div** tag. Assign it to the **class** slideshow-container. Inside it, get a **h1** tag. Inside the **h1** tag, put in any text you want. Add a **br** tag. Then open a **div** tag. Assign it to the **class** mySlides. You can add the **class** fade as well if you want to. Inside the **div** tag, get an **img** tag and the attribute **src** is the image path for the front cover of the book. Add a **style** attribute. Inside the **style** attribute, width should be set 200px and height is 200px as well. Add four **br** tags then open a **div** tag (as shown on line 172) and assign it to the **class** text. Add a **style** attribute and color can be set to blue (or any other colour you like!).

Then inside the **div** tag, enter the book's title, author and date of publication. Repeat two more times and close the starting **div** tag. Under it, add a **br** tag. Open another **div** tag and add a **style** attribute. In the **style** attribute, text-align should be set to center. Add three **span** tags and assign them to the **class** dot. Close the **div** and **center** tag. You can find out more about making slideshows at:

https://www.w3schools.com/howto/howto_js_slideshow.asp.

Open a **script** tag. Create a variable called `slideIndex` and set it to 0. Enter a `showSlides()` function. We will create that now.

```
201  function showSlides() {
202    var i;
203    var slides = document.getElementsByClassName("mySlides");
204    var dots = document.getElementsByClassName("dot");
205    for (i = 0; i < slides.length; i++) {
206      slides[i].style.display = "none";
207    }
208    slideIndex++;
209    if (slideIndex > slides.length) {slideIndex = 1}
210    for (i = 0; i < dots.length; i++) {
211      dots[i].className = dots[i].className.replace(" active", "");
212    }
213    slides[slideIndex-1].style.display = "block";
214    dots[slideIndex-1].className += " active";
215    setTimeout(showSlides, 5000); // Change image every 5 seconds
216  }
217  </script>
218      </body>
219  </html>
```

Figure 3-9: The last part of index.php

Create the function `showSlides()`. Inside it, create a variable called `i`. Create another one called `slides`. In the `slides` variable, type `document.getElementsByClassName("mySlides")`.

Now create another variable called `dots` and type `document.getElementsByClassName("dot")`. Create a for loop. In the brackets, enter `i = 0`, `i < slides.length` and `i++`. Inside the for loop, type `slides[i].style.display = "none"`. Close the for loop. Under the closing curly brackets, enter `slideIndex++`. Under it, open an if loop. In the brackets, enter `slideIndex > slides.length`. Inside the curly brackets, enter `slideIndex = 1`. Under that, create a for loop. In the brackets, enter `i = 0`, `i < dots.length` and `i++`. Inside the for loop, type `dots[i].className = dots[i].className.replace(" active", "")`. Close the curly brackets. Under it, type `slides[slideIndex-1].style.display = "block"` and `dots[slideIndex-1].className += " active"`.

Finally, enter `setTimeout(showSlides, 5000)`. This will change the image every five seconds. Close the **script** tag, the **body** tag and the **html** tag.

Creating our other project files

You can download the remaining project files from https://creativeproggrammer.atwebpages.com/source_a.php and https://creativeproggrammer.atwebpages.com/source_s.php.

Now we are going to create our other files.

First, we will begin by creating our files for the admin pages. Go to file manager and look for the directory named with your domain name. Then go into admin and create the following files:

```
respond.css
style.css
profile.png
add_book.php
add_student.php
admin_login.php
books.php
edit.php
expired.php
forgot.php
issue_info.php
logout.php
must.php
navbar.php
profile.php
student.php
```

Figure 3-10: The files we need to create for admin side

We now need to create our files for the student pages. Go to file manager and look for the directory named with your domain name. Then go into student and create the following files:

respond.css
style.css
profile.png
books.php
footer.php
issue_info.php
logout.php
navbar.php
search.php
student_login.php

Figure 3-11: The files we need for our student side

Now we have all the files we need. We can now start coding them!

Chapter 4: Admin Project Files

Download *style.css* and *respond.css*, since you will need them.

To check whether you have typed the right thing, you do not understand or you simply want the cheat sheet, you can download the code from:

http://creativeproggrammer.atwebpages.com/source_a.php.

Coding the navbar.php file

The first file we are going to start coding will be *navbar.php*. The techniques used will be shown in Chapter 7. First, you need to start a session, like this:

```php
<?php
  session_start();
?>
```

Figure 4-1: How to start a session

Then you need to declare the HTML document. Open the **html** and **head** tags. Leave the **title** tag empty, since we will include this in all the pages and the pages will already have a title. Use the **link** tag to link it to our *style.css* file. Then add links to Bootstrap. To find out more about Bootstrap, check out this site:

https://www.w3schools.com/bootstrap/default.asp. Figure 4-2 shows you the links.

```
<link rel="stylesheet" href="https://maxcdn.bootstrapcdn.com/bootstrap/3.3.7/css/bootstrap.min.css"
<script src="https://ajax.googleapis.com/ajax/libs/jquery/3.3.1/jquery.min.js"></script>
<script src="https://maxcdn.bootstrapcdn.com/bootstrap/3.3.7/js/bootstrap.min.js"></script>
```

Figure 4-2: How to link to Bootstrap

Close the **head** tag then open the **body** element. Now open a **nav** tag and assign it to the **class** navbar and navbar-inverse. These are Bootstrap classes. Open a **div** element and assign it to the **class** of container-fluid. Open another **div** tag and assign it to the

class of navbar-header. Open the **a** tag and give it the **class** of navbar-brand and active. Get the **style** attribute and in it, set **background-color** to #222. The text can be whatever you like! If you cannot think of anything, you can use Online Library Management System. Close the **div** tag and create an unordered list. Assign it to the **class** nav and navbar-nav. Open a **li** tag and inside add the **a** tag. The **href** attribute will have the link of **books.php**. The text will be *BOOKS*. Close the unordered list. Open a PHP tag (like you did before you started the session) and create an `if` loop. In the brackets, enter `isset($_SESSION['login_user'])`. Figure 4-3 shows you how.

```
<?php
   if(isset($_SESSION['login_user']))
   {?>
```

Figure 4-3: if loop

Create another unordered list and assign it to the **class** nav and navbar-nav. Open a **li** tag and inside it open the **a** tag. The **href** attribute will be set to **profile.php**. The text will be *EDIT PROFILE*. If you login at

http://creativeproggrammer.atwebpages.com/library/admin/admin_login.php and login, you can see the extra links that you do not see when you are not logged in.

Do the same thing, but the **href** attribute will link to **student.php** and the text will be *STUDENT-INFORMATION*.

Close the unordered list and create another unordered list. Type this code:

```
<li><a href="profile.php">
  <div style="color: white">

   <?php
     echo "<img class='img-circle profile_img' height=30 width=30 src='images/".$_SESSION['pic']."'>";
     echo " ".$_SESSION['login_user'];
   ?>
  </div>
</a></li>
```

Figure 4-4: What goes inside the next unordered list

The code in the PHP tags is to show the profile image and show you the user's username as shown in Figure 4-5.

Figure 4-5: What happens after you run the code in Figure 4-4

After, add a link to logout. Inside the **a** tag, before you add the word *LOGOUT*, get a **span** tag and assign it to the **class** glyphicon and glyphicon-log-out. For those of you that might already know a few glyphicon icons, you might have already guessed what icon it was. After the logout link, open a PHP tag and put an `else` condition. Figure 4-6 shows you what is inside the `else` condition.

```
    }
    else
    {    ?>
      <ul class="nav navbar-nav navbar-right">
        <li><a href="admin_login.php"><span class="glyphicon glyphicon-log-in"> LOGIN</span></a></li>
      </ul>
        <?php
    }
?>
```

Figure 4-6: Our else condition

The code in Figure 4-6 will show a link to login.

Create another unordered list and create a link to *admin_login.php* and use the login glyphicon **class**.

Close the **div** tag, close the **nav** tag, close the **body** tag and close the **html** tag.

Coding the admin_login.php file

First, you need to include our *connection.php* file and *navbar.php* file. Declare the HTML file, open a **html** tag and open a **head** tag. Add a **title** tag and inside it enter Admin Login. Add a **meta** tag with the same content as the one from your *navbar.php* file. Don't forget to add Bootstrap!

Close the **head** tag and open a **body** tag. Open a **section** tag and add a **style** attribute. Inside it, give it the height of 670px. Inside it, add a **div** tag and assign it to the **class** log_img. Add three **br** tags and open a **center** tag. Create a **div** tag and assign it to the **class** box1. Add the **br** tags inside it. Open a **h1** tag. Add the **style** attribute and set text-align to center. Set font-size to 35px and font-family to `Lucida Console`. The text will be Library Management System.

Add another **h1** tag underneath it. Add the same thing you put in the **style** attribute for the first **h1** tag but remove the font-family and change the font-size to 25px. Open a **form** tag and add the **name** attribute. In the **name** attribute, type `login`. Leave the **action** attribute empty and set the **method** attribute to `POST`. Inside the **form** tag, create a **div** tag and assign it to the **class** login.

Inside the **div** tag, create two **input** tags and assign them both to the **class** form-control. The first **input** tag will have the **type** attribute set to text and the second **input** tag will have the **type** attribute set to password. The first **input** will have the **name** attribute set to username and the second **input** set to password. The first **input** will have the **placeholder** attribute set to Username and the second to Password. Finally, set the **required** attribute to nothing. To find out more about **input** tags and forms, check out this site: https://www.w3schools.com/html/html_forms.asp.

Under the two **input** tags, open a **button** tag and assign it to the **class** btn and btn-default. The **type** attribute should be set to submit, and the **name** attribute should also be set to submit. The **value** attribute will be set to Login and then add a **style** attribute. In the **style** attribute, type `color: #429619; width: 70px; height: 30px;` and then close the **button** tag. Close the **div** tag and close the **form** tag. Open a **p** tag and enter the text Forgot your password. Then add the **a** tag and the **href** attribute to *forgot.php*. Add a **style** attribute and inside it set the color to yellow. The text will be Reset it. Close box1 and the **center** tag. Close the **div** tag and close the **section** tag.

Now open a PHP tag. Type `if(isset($_POST['submit']))` and in the curly brackets, create two variables called `username` and `password`. In both variables, type $_POST['username'] and $_POST['password'] to their corresponding variables. Create a variable called count and set it to 0. Create a variable called res. In the variable res, get a mysqli_query() function. Inside it, call your db variable and type SELECT * FROM `admin` WHERE username='$username'; then make a variable called row. Get the mysqli_fetch_assoc($res) function and create another variable called count. Get the function mysqli_num_rows($res) make an if condition, as shown in Figure 4-6.

```
if($count==0)
{
?>
<!--
<script>
  alert("The username and password don't exist.")
</script>
-->
<div class="alert alert-danger" style="width: 700px; margin-left: 360px; background-color: rgb(132, 57, 57); color: white; border
   <strong>The username and password don't exist.</strong>
</div>
<?php
}
```

Figure 4-6: if condition

The if condition above will give you an error if you enter the wrong username or password. Then add an else condition. Figure 4-7 below shows you what is inside the else condition.

```
else{
    /*------------------if username & password matches----------*/
    $_SESSION['login_user'] = $_POST['username'];
    $_SESSION['pic'] = $row['pic'];

    if(password_verify($password, $row['password'])) {
    ?>
    <script>
      window.location="profile.php";
    </script>
      <?php
}
if(mysqli_query($db, "SELECT * FROM `admin` WHERE username='$username' && password='$password';")) {
?>
<script>
    window.location="profile.php";
</script>
<?php
}
}
}
```

Figure 4-7: else condition

The else condition in Figure 4-7 will check whether the username and password match. Since the password is hashed, (you will find out more when we code ***must.php*** or you can see what it does at this site: https://www.php.net/manual/en/function.hash), it will say the password entered is wrong. So, the `password_verify` function will let you login. You can find out more at:

https://www.php.net/manual/en/function.password-verify. There is another if condition just in case the user has not changed their password yet, and it will still log them in. Then close the PHP tag, the **body** tag and the **html** tag.

Coding the profile.php file

Open a PHP tag and include our *connection.php* file and *navbar.php* file. Declare the HTML file, open a **html** tag, open a **head** tag and open a **title** tag. Inside the **title** tag, give the page a title such as Edit Profile or Your Profile. Add the **meta** tag we have added in the other files we have coded so far. Add the Bootstrap links and then open the **body** tag. Add a **style** attribute and set background-color to white. Create a **div** tag and assign it to the Bootstrap class container.

Add a **form** tag and set the **method** attribute to POST. Inside the **form** tag, add a **button** element and assign it to the **class** btn and btn-default. Add a **style** attribute. In the **style** attribute, set float to right, background-color to #f3f402 and width to 70px. Add the **name** attribute and set it to submit1. Then add the **type** attribute and set it to submit. The text will be Edit and close the **button** tag. Close the **form** tag and open a **div** tag. Assign the **div** tag to the **class** wrapper. Then open a PHP tag and create an if condition.

Type `if(isset($_POST['submit1']))` then close the PHP tag. Open the **script** tag then in the **script** tag, type `window.location="edit.php";` and open another PHP tag then close the if condition. Then create a variable called q and put inside it `mysqli_query($db, "SELECT * FROM admin WHERE username='$_SESSION[login_user]' ;")`. Close the PHP tag and get a **h2** tag. Add the **style** attribute and inside it, text-align will be set to center. The text inside the tag will be Staff Info. Open another PHP tag and create a variable called `row`. Put a `mysqli_fetch_assoc($q)` function inside this variable. Get an `if` condition.

In the brackets, enter `$row['login'] == "no"`. This will check whether the column login is equals to yes or no. Close the PHP tag and then get a **div** tag. Assign it to the **class** alert. Inside the **div** tag, open a **p** tag. Put the text: 'Please change your password' and then add the **a** tag. The **href** attribute will be set to ***must.php***, and the text inside the **a** tag will be 'Click here to change it'. Open the PHP tag again.

Close the curly brackets from our `if` condition. Figure 4-8 shows you what goes inside the `echo`.

```
echo "<div style='text-align: center;'>
<img class='img-circle profile_img' height='110' width='120' src='images/".$_SESSION['pic']."'>
</div>";
```

Figure 4-8: Inside the echo

This code will show the user their profile image. Close the PHP tag then open a **div** tag. Add a **style** attribute and inside it, set **text-align** to center. Inside the **div** tag, add a **strong** tag and inside it the text will be 'Welcome'. Add a **h4** tag. Then open a single line PHP tag (where the opening and closing PHP tags are on one line) and inside this tag add an `echo` and add `$_SESSION['login_user']`. Close the **h4** tag and close the **div** tag. Then open a PHP tag. Add `echo` and inside, add a **b** tag. Add another `echo` and add a **table** tag inside. Assign it to the **class** table and table-bordered. Add another `echo` and put a **tr** tag inside it. Add another with a **td** tag in it. Add another `echo` with a **b** tag and the text inside will be Username. Add another `echo` and inside it add a closing **td** tag. Do the same thing again. The only difference is, where you typed Username, replace it with: `$row['username']`. Figure 4-9 shows you what it does.

Figure 4-9: What profile.php does

Figure 4-9 shows the outcome when the user has not changed their password yet. The alert box does not show if the user has already changed their password.

Close the PHP tag, the two **div** tags, the **body** tag and the **html** tag.

Coding the must.php file

Open a PHP tag and include our ***connection.php*** file and ***navbar.php*** file. Declare the document, open the **html** tag and open the **head** tag. In the **head** tag, add a **title** tag. In the **title** tag, set the title to 'Change your password'. Add the **meta** tag we have put in other pages and add Bootstrap links. Close the **head** element and open the **body** tag. Add the **style** attribute to the body tag. In the **style** attribute, set background-color to white, color to blue and text-align to center. Open a **h2** tag.

Add the **style** attribute and set text-align to center. The text will be 'Change your password'. Open a PHP tag and create a variable called `sql`. In the variable, it will be `SELECT * FROM admin WHERE username='$_SESSION[login_user]'`. Create another variable called `result`. In the variable, add the function `mysqli_query($db, $sql)`. Add a `while` loop. In the brackets for the `while` loop, create a variable called `row` and add the function `mysqli_fetch_assoc($result)`.

In the curly brackets, create two variables called `username` and `password`. In these two variables, type `$row['username']` and `$row['password']`, to their corresponding variables. Close the curly brackets, close the PHP tags and open a **div** tag. Assign it to the **class** profile_info. Inside the **div** element, open a **span** tag. Inside the **span** tag, the text will be Welcome. Close the **span** tag. Open a **h4** tag. Open a single line PHP tag, where the opening and closing tag is on the same line. In the PHP tags, add an `echo`. Inside the `echo`, check whether the admin is logged in, then close the PHP tag and close the **h4** tag.

Close the **div** tag and add two **br** tags. Open a **div** tag and open a **form** tag. Set the **method** attribute to POST. Inside the **form** tag, add a **label** tag, inside it, add a **h4** tag and inside the **h4** tag, add a **b** tag. The text in this tag will be Password. Underneath it, open a **center** tag, and inside it, add an **input** tag. Set the **type** attribute to password, set the **name** attribute to pass1 and set the **placeholder** attribute to New Password. Close the **center** tag.

Repeat the above but change the text in the **b** tag to 'Confirm Password', set the **name** attribute to pass2 and set the **placeholder** attribute to Confirm Password. Open a **div** tag and add a **style** attribute. In the **style** attribute, set padding-left to 10px. Inside the **div** tag, open a **button** tag. Assign it to the **class** btn and btn-default. Add the **style** attribute and set color to green. The **type** attribute will be set to submit, the **name** attribute should be set to save or submit, and the text will be Save Your Profile. The PHP code in Figure 4-10 processes the form, hashes the password, checks whether the passwords match and update the admin table.

```php
<?php
    if(isset($_POST['save']))
    {
            $pass1=$_POST['pass1'];
            $pass2=$_POST['pass2'];

            if($pass1 != $pass2) {
                echo "<script>alert('The passwords do not match!')</script>";
                echo "<script>window.location='must.php'</script>";
            }

            if($pass1 == $pass2) {
    $options = array("cost"=>4);
        $hash = password_hash($pass1,PASSWORD_BCRYPT,$options);

    $sql1= "UPDATE `admin` SET `password`='$hash', `login`='yes' WHERE `username`='".$_SESSION['login_user']."'";";

    if(mysqli_query($db,$sql1))
    {
        ?>
        <script>
            alert("Your New Password was saved succesfully!");
            window.location="profile.php";
        </script>
        <?php
    }
    }
    }
?>
```

Figure 4-10: The PHP code to process the form

Close the **body** and **html** tag.

Coding the edit.php file

This page is the same as *must.php*. But instead of changing your password, you can change your username, password and profile image.

Coding our books.php file

This is the biggest file in the project. As we have done previously, start by including the connection and navbar file, declaring the document and adding starting tags. After opening the **body** tag, the first thing we are going to add is the sidenav. The sidenav will take us to two more pages that are not in the horizontal navbar. Figure 4-11 shows you how it looks.

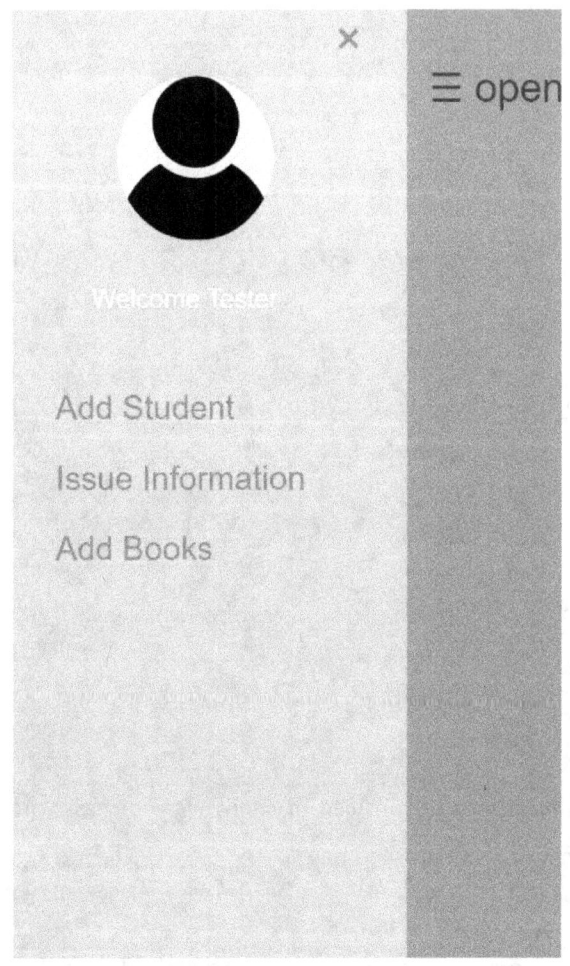

Figure 4-11: How the sidenav looks

Or you can cheat from here: https://www.w3schools.com/howto/howto_js_sidenav.asp

Figure 4-12 shows you how to code the sidenav.

```
<!--_____sidenav_____-->

   <div id="mySidenav" class="sidenav" style="text-decoration: none;">
   <a href="javascript:void(0)" class="closebtn" onclick="closeNav()" style="text-decoration: none;">&times;</a>

                  <div style="color: white; margin-left: 60px; font-size: 20px;">
                  <?php
                  if(isset($_SESSION['login_user']))
                     { echo "<img class='img-circle profile_img' height=120 width=120 src='images/".$_SESSION['pic']."'>";
                     echo "</br></br>";

                        echo "Welcome ".$_SESSION['login_user'];
                     }
                  ?>
                  </div><br><br>

   <div class="pop">  <a href="add_student.php" style="text-decoration: none;">Add Student</a> </div>
   <div class="pop">  <a href="issue_info.php" style="text-decoration: none;">Issue Information</a> </div>
   <div class="pop">  <a href="add_books.php" style="text-decoration: none;">Add Books</a></div>
   </div>

   <div id="main">
      <span style="font-size:30px;cursor:pointer" onclick="openNav()">&#9776; open</span>

<script>
function openNav() {
   document.getElementById("mySidenav").style.width = "300px";
   document.getElementById("main").style.marginLeft = "300px";
   document.body.style.backgroundColor = "rgba(0,0,0,0.4)";
}

function closeNav() {
   document.getElementById("mySidenav").style.width = "0";
   document.getElementById("main").style.marginLeft = "0";
   document.body.style.backgroundColor = "white";
```

Figure 4-12: The code for the sidenav – don't forget to close the curly brackets and script tag!

Open a **div** tag and assign it to the **class** srch. Inside it, open a **form** tag and assign it to the **class** navbar-form. Set the **method** attribute to POST and **name** attribute to form1. Inside it, add an **input** tag. Set the **name** attribute to search and set the **placeholder** attribute to 'Search for a book'. Underneath it, open a **button** tag and add the **style** attribute. Set the background-color to light green. Set the **type** attribute to submit. Also set the **name** attribute to submit. Assign it to the **class** btn and btn-default. In the **button** tag, open a **span** tag and assign it to the **class** glyphicon and glyphicon-search. Close the **span** tag, close the **button** tag and add two **br** tags.

Close the **form** tag and open another **form** tag. Copy the form attributes from form1. Just name this form form2. Change the **input** tag **name** attribute to bid and **placeholder** attribute to 'Search for a Book ID'. Remove the **span** tag in the **button** tag and replace it with the words 'Delete a Book'. Change the button's **name** attribute to delete. Close this **form** tag and add a **p** tag. Assign it to the **class** demo. Close the **div** tag and open the PHP tag. Add an `if` condition and check if the button named submit has been clicked using the `isset()` function, like we have done before. Inside the curly brackets, create a variable called q. Inside the variable, type

```
mysqli_query($db, "SELECT * FROM  books WHERE title LIKE
'%$_POST[search]%' ").
```

Add an `if` condition and in the brackets type `mysqli_num_rows($q)==0`. In the curly brackets, add an `echo`. In the quotation marks, write: Sorry, I did not get that. Try checking: **br** tag 1. Spelling **br** tag 2. Try another phrase **br** tag 3. The book does not exist. Close the curly brackets then add an `else` condition. Figure 4-13 shows you how to make a table with PHP.

```php
echo "<table class='table table-bordered table-hover'>";
// Table rows(tr)
echo "<tr style='background-color: lightgreen;'>";
// Table header(th)
echo "<th>"; echo "ID"; echo "</th>";
echo "<th>"; echo "ISBN No."; echo "</th>";
echo "<th>"; echo "Title"; echo "</th>";
echo "<th>"; echo "Author(s)"; echo "</th>";
echo "<th>"; echo "Publisher"; echo "</th>";
echo "<th>"; echo "Status"; echo "</th>";
echo "<th>"; echo "Quantity"; echo "</th>";
echo "<th>"; echo "Section"; echo "</th>";

echo "</tr>";

while($row=mysqli_fetch_assoc($q))
{
echo "<tr>";
// Table data(td)
echo "<td>"; echo $row['bid']; echo "</td>";
echo "<td>"; echo $row['isbn']; echo "</td>";
echo "<td>"; echo $row['title']; echo "</td>";
echo "<td>"; echo $row['authors']; echo "</td>";
echo "<td>"; echo $row['publisher']; echo "</td>";
echo "<td>"; echo $row['status']; echo "</td>";
echo "<td>"; echo $row['quantity']; echo "</td>";
echo "<td>"; echo $row['section']; echo "</td>";

echo "</tr>";
}
```

Figure 4-13: The code for our books table in PHP

Copy the slideshow from *index.php* (outside the *library* directory) but change the **h1** tag to Favourite Books. Close the curly brackets, close the PHP tag, close the **body** tag and close the **html** tag.

Coding the add_books.php file

Include the connection file, include the navbar, declare the document, open the **html** tag, the **head** tag and **title** tag. The title will be 'Add Books'. Add the **meta** tag, close the **head** tag and open the **body** element. Open the **h2** tag and add the **style** attribute. Set text-align to center. Close the **h2** tag and open a **div** tag. Inside the **div** tag, open a **form**

tag and set the **method** attribute to POST. Inside this form, open a **label** tag, add a **style** attribute and set text-align to center.

The text will be 'Front Cover Image Upload'. Add a **center** tag and inside, add the **input** tag. Assign it to the **class** form-control. Set the **type** attribute to file and also set the **name** attribute to file. Close the **center** tag, add a **br** tag and open another **center** tag. Inside the **center** tag, add another **input** tag, set the **type** attribute to text and **name** attribute to isbn. Assign it to the **class** form-control and set the **placeholder** to ISBN No. Close the **center** tag and add a **br** tag.

Repeat the above six times. The other **name** attributes will be title, authors, publisher, status, quantity and section. The **name** attributes will be the same as the **placeholder** attributes. Open another **center** tag and inside it, open a **textarea** tag. Assign it to the **class** form-control, set the **name** attribute and **placeholder** attribute to description and the **type** attribute to text. Close the **textarea** tag, close the **center** tag and add a **br** tag.

Open a **div** tag and add the **style** attribute. In the **style** attribute, set padding-left to 10px. Inside the **div** tag, open a **center** tag then open a **button** element. Assign it to the **class** btn and btn-default. Add the **style** attribute and set the color to green. Set the **type** attribute to submit and set the **name** attribute to add. The text will be 'Add Books'. Close the **button** tag, **center** tag and **div** tag. Then add two **br** elements. Close the **form** tag, close the **div** tag and open the PHP tag. The PHP code in Figure 4-14 is to add the books to database.

```php
if(isset($_SESSION['login_user'])){

    if(isset($_POST['add']))
    {

    move_uploaded_file($_FILES['file']['tmp_name'], "images/".$_FILES['file']['name']);

    $isbn=$_POST['isbn'];
    $title=$_POST['title'];
    $authors=$_POST['authors'];
    $publisher=$_POST['publisher'];
    $status=$_POST['status'];
    $quantity=$_POST['quantity'];
    $section=$_POST['section'];
    $description=mysqli_real_escape_string($_POST['description']);
    $image=$_FILES['file']['name'];

    $sql= "INSERT INTO books (`isbn`, `title`, `authors`, `publisher`, `status`, `quantity`, `section`, `description`, `image`) VALUES ('$isbn',

    if(mysqli_query($db,$sql) or die(mysqli_error($db)))
    {
        ?>
            <script>
                alert("Book added successfully!");
            </script>
        <?php
    }
    }
}
```

Figure 4-14: The PHP code to add the book to the database

Close the PHP tag, the **body** tag and the **html** tag.

Coding the add_student.php file

The *add_student.php* file will be the same as *add_books.php* but change the form to match the columns in the database. So, you can check the student table for the columns and then change the form and PHP for it to work correctly.

Coding the logout.php file

Open the PHP tag, start a session and add an `if` condition. Type `isset($_SESSION['login_user'])` and in the curly brackets, type `unset($_SESSION['login_user'])`. Close the curly brackets then add a `header` with the location of *admin_login.php*.

Coding the forgot.php file

You can copy the code from *admin_login.php* but add an extra **input** tag. The **input** tag names will be username, email and password. The text for the submit button is 'Update'. This is the PHP code:

```php
<?php
    if(isset($_POST['submit']))
    {
    $options = array("cost"=>4);
    $hash = password_hash($_POST['password'],PASSWORD_BCRYPT,$options);
        if(mysqli_query($db,"UPDATE admin SET password='$hash' WHERE username='$_POST[username]'
        AND email='$_POST[email]' ;"))
        {
            ?>
                    <script type="text/javascript">
    alert("The Password Updated Successfully.");
    </script>
                    <?php
        }
    }
?></div>
```

Figure 4-15: The PHP code for forgot.php

The PHP code in Figure 4-15 will update the user's password.

Coding the issue_info.php file

Open the PHP tag, include the connection file, the navbar file and declare the HTML file. Open the **html** tag and **head** tag. In the **head** tag, add a **title** tag. In the **title** tag, type 'Borrow Information'. Add the usual **meta** tag. Add the sidenav then open a **div** tag. Assign it to the **class** container. Inside the **div** tag, add a **h3** tag and add the **style** attribute. In the **style** attribute, set **text-align** to center and **font-weight** to bold. Open a PHP tag and create a variable called c. The variable will be equal to 0. Add an if condition and type isset($_SESSION['login_user']) in the brackets. Create another variable called sql. Inside it, type SELECT student.username,id,books.bid,title,authors,publisher,borrow_date,return_date FROM student INNER JOIN issue_book ON student.username=issue_book.username INNER JOIN books ON issue_book.bid=books.bid WHERE issue_book.approve ='Borrowed' ORDER BY `issue_book`.`return_date` ASC.

Create another variable called res. Inside the variable, add the function mysqli_query($db, $sql). Then add an echo and inside the quotation marks, add a **div** tag. Assign it to the **class** scroll. Then add another echo and open a **table** tag. Assign them to the **class** table and table-bordered. Add a **style** attribute and set width to 100%. Add another echo with a **tr** tag inside the quotation marks. Add the

style attribute and set **background-color** to black and the **color** to white. Add twenty-seven `echo`s, with three `echo`s on each line. In the first `echo` on each line, add an opening **th** tag and in the last `echo` on each line add a closing **th** tag. In the second `echo` on each line, type this text in this order: Username, Library ID, Book ID, ISBN Number, Book Title, Authors, Publisher, Borrow Date and Return Date. Close the **tr** tag.

Add a `while` loop and in the brackets, create a variable called `row`. In the variable `row`, add the function `mysqli_fetch_assoc($res)`. In the curly brackets, create a variable called `d`. In this variable, you're going to call the PHP function `date()` and in the brackets, enter `Y-m-d`, in quotation marks. Get an `if` condition. In the brackets, call the variable `d` and check whether it is greater than `$row['return_date']`. In the curly brackets, create a variable called `c` and inside the variable, type `c+1`. Create a variable called `var`. In this variable, add a **p** tag. In the **p** tag, add a **style** attribute. Set **color** to yellow and **background-color** to red. The text in the **p** tag will be EXPIRED. Add a `mysqli_query($db,` "UPDATE issue_book SET approve='$var' WHERE \`return_date\`='$row[return_date]' and approve='Yes' LIMIT $c;"); then add an `echo`. In the quotation marks, type `$d."<br>"`. Close the curly brackets.

```
echo "<td>"; echo $row['username']; echo "</td>";
echo "<td>"; echo $row['id']; echo "</td>";
echo "<td>"; echo $row['bid']; echo "</td>";
echo "<td>"; echo $row['isbn']; echo "</td>";
echo "<td>"; echo $row['title']; echo "</td>";
echo "<td>"; echo $row['authors']; echo "</td>";
echo "<td>"; echo $row['publisher']; echo "</td>";
echo "<td>"; echo $row['borrow_date']; echo "</td>";
echo "<td>"; echo $row['return_date']; echo "</td>";
```

Figure 4-16: The twenty-seven echos

Type the code that is demonstrated in Figure 4-16.

Add an `else` condition. Close the PHP tag, and add a **h3** tag. Add a **style** attribute. In the **style** attribute, **text-align** is set to center and **font-weight** is set to bold. The text in the **h3** tag is: 'You MUST login before you can see the information of borrowed book's.

Close the **h3** tag, open another PHP tag and close the curly brackets. Close the PHP tag, the two **div** tags, the **body** tag and the **html** tag.

Coding the expired.php file

As previously, start by including the connection file, navbar file, declaring the document, open the **html** tag and **head** tag. Give the page the title of 'Expired Books'. Add the sidenav. After you have added the sidenav, add a **div** element and assign it to the **class** container. Open a PHP tag and add an `if` condition. In the brackets, type `$_SESSION['login_user']` and close the PHP tag. Add a **div** tag and assign it to the **class** srch. Add a **br** tag and open a **form** tag. Set the **method** attribute to POST and set the **name** attribute to form1. Add two **input** tags. One will be called username and the other will be called bid. Which means, the placeholder of one will be username and another will be bid.

Add a **button** tag and assign it to the **class** btn and btn-default. Set the **name** attribute to submit and also set the **name** attribute to submit. Close the **button** tag and add two **br** tags. Close the **form** tag and the **div** tag. Open the PHP tag and create an `if` condition. In the brackets, type `isset($_POST['submit'])`. In the curly brackets, create a variable called `var1`. In this variable, add a **p** element and add the **style** attribute. In the **style** attribute, set color to yellow and background-color to green. The text in the **p** tag is RETURNED.

Add a `mysqli_query($db, "UPDATE issue_book SET approve='$var1' WHERE username='$_POST[username]' AND bid='$_POST[bid]' ")`. Add another `mysqli_query($db, "UPDATE`

```
books SET status='Available' AND quantity = quantity+1
WHERE bid='$_POST[bid]' ").
```
Close the two curly brackets. Create a variable called c and set it to 0. Create `ret`, `exp`, `sql3` and `res3`. In the variable `ret`, add a

p tag and add the **style** attribute. In the **style** attribute, set color to yellow and background-color to green.

The text in the **p** tag will be RETURNED. Do the same for the variable `exp`, except that the background-color will be set to red and the text will be EXPIRED. In the variable `sql3`, type

```
SELECT
student.username,id,books.bid,title,authors,publisher,appr
ove,borrow_date,return_date FROM student inner join
issue_book ON student.username=issue_book.username inner
join books ON issue_book.bid=books.bid WHERE
issue_book.approve ='$exp' and issue_book.approve ='$ret'
ORDER BY `issue_book`.`return_date` DESC.
```
Finally, in the variable `res3`, add a `mysqli_query($db, $sql3)`

which will run the variable `sql3`. Add an `echo` and inside it open the **table** tag. Assign it to the **class** table and table-bordered. Add the **style** attribute.

In the **style** attribute, set width to 100%. The table we made to show the issue information in *issue_info.php*, you can copy it here. But the variable in the `while` loop will be `res3`. Once you've done that, close the PHP tag, close the two **div** tags, close the **body** tag and close the **html** tag.

Chapter 5: Student Project Files

Download *style.css* and *respond.css*, since you will need them.

To check whether you have typed the right thing, you do not understand or you simply want the cheat sheet, you can download the code from:

http://creativeproggrammer.atwebpages.com/source_s.php or go to Chapter 7.

Coding the navbar.php file

You can copy and paste the navbar.php file from admin side; the only difference is, you remove the profile link and the extra links that admin see. The two following figures show you how it works. Also, Figure 5-3 shows you the PHP at the top of the navbar.php file for student side.

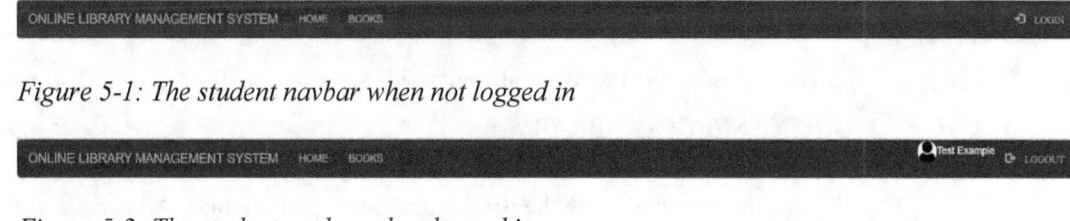

Figure 5-1: The student navbar when not logged in

ONLINE LIBRARY MANAGEMENT SYSTEM   HOME   BOOKS   Test Example   LOGOUT

Figure 5-2: The student navbar when logged in

```
$user = $_SESSION['login_user'];
$get_user = "SELECT * FROM student WHERE username='$user'";
$run_user = mysqli_query($db, $get_user);
$row = mysqli_fetch_array($run_user);

$first = $row['first'];
$last = $row['last'];
```

Figure 5-3: The extra code at the top of navbar.php

The two navbars look the same, right? But the difference is that in Figure 5-2, the LOGIN link is a LOGOUT link and that before the LOGOUT link, there is the student's full name and profile image (all students will have the same profile image). The HOME link will be linked to index.php, the BOOKS link to books.php, the

LOGIN link to student_login.php and the LOGOUT link to logout.php. The image profile link will not be linked to anywhere.

Under the `echo` where we call to show the profile image, add another `echo` and inside the quotation, call the variables starting with `first`, a space, then, `last`.

Coding the index.php file

This page is the home page for student side. First, start a session, declare the document, open the **html** element and open the **head** element. Inside the **head** tag, open a **title** tag. The title of this page will be 'School Library Management System'. Close the **title** tag and add the **meta** tag we added on admin pages files. Do not include Bootstrap. Close the **head** tag, open a **body** tag and open a **div** tag. Assign it to the **class** wrapper. Inside it, add a **header** tag. Add the **style** attribute. Set width to 100%. Inside it, open a **div** tag and assign it to the **class** logo. Inside this **div** element, add two **br** tags and an **Img** tag. Assign it to the **class** shake. Add the width and height attributes. Set both attributes to 90. Set the **src** attribute to *images/open.png*. add a **h1** tag and assign it to the **class** glow. Add the **style** attribute and set color to light green. The text will be 'ONLINE SCHOOL LIBRARY'.

Close the **h1** element, close the **div** tag and open the PHP tags. Add an `if` condition. In the brackets, type `isset($_SESSION['login_user'])`. Open the curly brackets and close the PHP tags. Open a **nav** tag. Inside it, open an unordered list. Inside that, add three **li** tags with the **a** tags inside them. The first **li** tag will be a link to *index.php* and the text will be HOME. The second **li** tag will be a link to *books.php* and the text will be BOOKS. The final one will be a link to *logout.php* and the text will be LOGOUT. Close the unordered list, close the **nav** tag and open the PHP tag. In the PHP tag, close the curly brackets and add an `else` condition. Close the PHP tag. Open another **nav** element and inside, add another unordered list. Copy what you did in the first unordered list, changing the logout link to *student_login.php* and the text to LOGIN or STUDENT-LOGIN. Close the unordered list, close the **nav** tag and open the PHP tag. Close the curly brackets and close the PHP tag. Close the **header** tag and open a **section** tag. Add the **style** attribute and set width to 1000%. Open a **div** tag and assign it to the **class** sec_img.

Add the **style** attribute and set position to relative. Inside it, add a **center** tag and inside the **center** tag, add an **img** tag. Assign it to the **class** shake and img. Add the **width** and

height attributes and set them both to 200. Assign to the **id** 3. Find an image and link it to the **src** attribute. Add three **br** tags and open a **div** tag. Assign it to the **class** box. Inside it, add four **br** tags then open a **h1** tag. Add the **style** attribute. Inside the **style** attribute, set text-align to center and font-size to 35px. The text will be Welcome to Online School Library. Add two **br** tags and close the two **div** tags, close the **section** tag and close the **div** tag. Open a PHP tag and include *footer.php*. Close the PHP tag, close the **body** tag and close the **html** tag.

Coding the logout.php file

Copy the *logout.php* file from admin section but changing the `header` location to *index.php* instead.

Coding the footer.php file

Declare the file, open the **html** tag, open the **head** tag and leave the **title** tag empty. Add the **meta** tag. For how to code the social media icons, look here: https://www.w3schools.com/howto/howto_css_social_media_buttons.asp.

Put the styling in the **style** tag, the Font Awesome link in the **head** tag and put the icons at the bottom of the footer file. Before you add the social media icons, add a **h3** tag. The text inside the **h3** element is Email: example@example.com Contact us through social media Contact: 01234567891.

Coding the student_login.php file

Copy the login from admin section, changing the table to student and changing the title to Student Login. Remove the `password_verify()` function.

Coding the books.php file

Include the connection file, include the navbar file, then include this code:

```
$ms = "SELECT * FROM student WHERE username='$_SESSION[login_user]'";
$d = mysqli_query($db, $ms);
$rows = mysqli_fetch_assoc($d);

$first = $rows['first'];
$last = $rows['last'];
$name = "Welcome, ".$first." ".$last;
```

Figure 5-4: The PHP code at the top of our books.php file

Close the PHP tag and declare the file. Open the **html** tag and the **head** tag. Add a **title** tag and set the title to Books. Add the **meta** tag, the Bootstrap links and close the **head** tag. Open the **body** tag then add the sidenav. You can copy the sidenav from admin section. In the sidenav from admin section, where it says welcome in an `echo`, replace it with the variable `name`.

Copy the search and delete form from admin side. Change the delete form to a reservation form. The reservation button's name attribute will be reserve, and the text will be Reserve a Book. Close the **form** tag and close the **div** tag. Open the PHP tag. Add an `if` condition where it checks whether the search submit button. Inside the curly brackets, include the file *search.php*. Create a variable called `books`. Inside it, type SELECT * FROM books WHERE title LIKE'%$_POST[search]%'. Create another variable called `run` and get the function `mysqli_query($db, $books)`. Create a variable called `rows` and add the function `mysqli_fetch_array($run)`. Create the following variables: `bid`, `isbn`, `btitle`, `bauthor`, `bpublisher`, `quantity`, `bsection`, `description`, `bimage`. Inside these variables, type the following to their corresponding variables:

```
$rows['bid'],          $rows['isbn'],          $rows['btitle'],
$rows['bauthor'], $rows['bpublisher'],
```

```
$rows['quantity'],   $rows['section'],   $rows['description'],
$rows['image'].
```

In the table showing you search results, where the table row where it shows you the book's title, open a **button** element and add the **id** attribute. The **id** attribute will be set to open. Assign it to the **class** btn and btn-info. The text will be Preview.

To cheat for this part, check out:
https://www.w3schools.com/howto/howto_css_modals.asp.

Complete Web Applications using PHP and MySQL

Build a Library Management System for   Complete Web Applications
your school.   using PHP and MySQL cover

Book ID: 1

ISBN No.: 9781652770459

Section: Computers/Web/Non-Fiction

Quantity: 1

Publisher:

By

Figure 5-5: What happens when you click the preview button

The code for the modal is in Figure 5-6 and 5-7. It uses the variables we made above show, which is why you get the outcome in Figure 5-5.

```
                 echo "<!-- The Modal -->
<div id='myModal' class='modal'>

  <!-- Modal content -->
  <center><div class='modal-content' style='width: 500px;'>
    <div style='background-color: lightgreen;' class='modal-header'>
      <span style='color: black; background-color: grey; padding-left: 3px; padding-right: 3px; padding-bottom: 3px; padding-top: 3px;' class
      <h2>$btitle</h2>
    </div>
    <div class='modal-body'>
      <img src='$bimage' width=210 height=300 alt='$btitle cover' style='float: right;'>
      <p>$description</p>
      <p>Book ID: $bid</p>
      <p>ISBN No.: $isbn</p>
      <p>Section: $bsection</p>
      <p>Quantity: $quantity</p>
      <p>Publisher: $bpublisher</p>
      <div class='modal-footer'>
        <h3>By $bauthor</h3>
      </div>
    </div></center>

</div>
<script>
// Get the modal
var modal = document.getElementById('myModal');

// Get the button that opens the modal
var btn = document.getElementById('open');

// Get the <span> element that closes the modal
var span = document.getElementsByClassName('close')[0];

// When the user clicks the button, open the modal
btn.onclick = function() {
  modal.style.display = 'block';
}
```

Figure 5-6: The code for the modal box

```
// When the user clicks on <span> (x), close the modal
span.onclick = function() {
  modal.style.display = 'none';
}

// When the user clicks anywhere outside of the modal, close it
window.onclick = function(event) {
  if (event.target == modal) {
    modal.style.display = 'none';
  }
}
</script>
";
```

Figure 5-7: The rest of the JavaScript

You will put the code in Figure 5-6 and 5-7 under where the search results table closes. The code in Figure 5-8 is to reserve the book.

```
if(isset($_SESSION['login_user'])) {
    if(isset($_POST['reserve'])) {
        $query = "INSERT INTO issue_book VALUES('', '$_SESSION[login_user]', '$_POST[bid]', 'Yes', NOW(), NOW() + INTERVAL 35 DAY)";
        $quant = "UPDATE books SET status='Not Available', quantity=quantity-1 WHERE books.bid=$_POST[bid]";
        $run = mysqli_query($db, $query);
        $run2 = mysqli_query($db, $quant);
    }
```

Figure 5-8: The code for what happens when you click the reserve button

Coding the search.php file

The code in Figure 5-9 will run what happens when you search for a book.

```php
<?php
$search_query = $_POST['search'];
  $q=mysqli_query($db,"SELECT * FROM books WHERE title LIKE'%$_POST[search]%'");
  $books = "SELECT * FROM books WHERE title LIKE'%$_POST[search]%'";
    $run = mysqli_query($db, $books);
    $rows = mysqli_fetch_array($run);
?>
```

Figure 5-9: The code in search.php

Coding the issue_book.php file

Add the PHP code you put at the top of *books.php*. Copy the sidenav from *books.php*. Copy the rest of the *issue_book.php* file from the admin section. The sql variable will be different though. The difference is shown here:

Admin Section sql variable:

SELECT
student.username,id,books.bid,title,authors,publisher,borr
ow_date,return_date FROM student INNER JOIN issue_book ON
student.username=issue_book.username INNER JOIN books ON
issue_book.bid=books.bid WHERE issue_book.approve
='Borrowed' ORDER BY `issue_book`.`return_date` ASC.

Student Section sql variable:

SELECT
student.username,id,books.bid,title,authors,publisher,appr
ove,borrow_date,return_date FROM student inner join
issue_book ON student.username=issue_book.username inner
join books ON issue_book.bid=books.bid WHERE
issue_book.username ='$_SESSION[login_user]' AND

```
issue_book.approve !='' ORDER BY
`issue_book`.`return_date` ASC.
```

The differences are that in the admin section variable, it looks for the books that have not expired or been returned and shows borrowed books data for all the students. In the student section variable, it looks for all the books in the issue_book table and it checks which user is logged in, only showing the books that the user logged in has borrowed.

Chapter 6: Techniques

In this chapter, I will explain each technique, add screenshots and give you extra links to look at.

1. `$_SESSION['login_user']`

This checks whether a user is logged in this project.

```
$_SESSION['login_user']
```

Figure 6-1: The code to check whether a user is logged in

2. `mysqli_query()`

This function runs a SQL query. Find out more at:
https://www.php.net/manual/en/mysqli.query.php.

```
mysqli_query
```

Figure 6-2: mysqli_query()

3. `mysqli_fetch_assoc()`

Returns an associative array that corresponds to the fetched row or NULL if there are no more rows. Find out more at: https://www.php.net/manual/en/mysqli-result.fetch-assoc.php.

```
mysqli_fetch_assoc
```

Figure 6-3: mysqli_fetch_assoc

4. `mysqli_num_rows()`

Returns the number of rows in the result set. Find out more at:

https://www.php.net/manual/en/mysqli-result.num-rows.php.

mysqli_num_rows

Figure 6-4: mysqli_num_rows

5. `mysqli_connect()`

Connects to the database. Find out more at:

https://www.php.net/manual/en/function.mysqli-connect.php

mysqli_connect

Figure 6-5: mysqli_connect

6. `date()`

Format a local time/date. Find out more at:

https://www.php.net/manual/en/function.date

Chapter 7: The Complete Project Code

In this final chapter, I have put together all the code. You can check whether you have entered the right thing and each page has how it looks. All the screenshots are from the demo.

Admin Section

Here is all the code for admin section. The first code is for *admin_login.php*:

```php
<?php

    include "connection.php";

    include "navbar.php";

?>
<!DOCTYPE html>

<html>

    <head>

        <title>

            Admin Login

        </title>

        <link rel="stylesheet" href="css/style.css">

        <link rel="stylesheet" href="css/respond.css">

        <meta charset="utf-8">

        <meta name="viewport" content="width=device-width,
initial-scale=1.0">

<meta http-equiv="X-UA-Compatible"
content="IE=edge,chrome=1">

<meta name="HandheldFriendly" content="true">
```

```
<link rel="stylesheet"
href="https://maxcdn.bootstrapcdn.com/bootstrap/3.4.0/css/
bootstrap.min.css">

<script
src="https://ajax.googleapis.com/ajax/libs/jquery/3.4.0/jq
uery.min.js"></script>

<script
src="https://maxcdn.bootstrapcdn.com/bootstrap/3.4.0/js/bo
otstrap.min.js"></script>

    </head>

<body>

    <section style="height: 670px;">

        <div class="log_img">

            <br><br><br>

            <center><div class="box1">

                <br><br>

                    <h1 style="text-align: center; font-
size: 35px; font-family: Lucida Console;">Library
Management System</h1><br>

                    <h1 style="text-align: center; font-
size: 25px;">Staff Login</h1>

                    <form name="login" action=""
method="post">

                    <div class="login">

                        <input class="form-control"
type="text" name="username" placeholder="Username"
required=""><br>

                        <input class="form-control"
type="password" name="password" placeholder="Password"
required=""><br>

                        <input class="btn btn-default"
type="submit" name="submit" value="Login" style="color:
#429619; width: 70px; height: 30px;">
```

```
</div>

</form>

            <p>Forgot your Password?<a
href="forgot.php" style="color: yellow;"> Reset it</a></p>

            </div></center>

        </div>

    </section>

    <?php

      if(isset($_POST['submit']))

      {

      $username = $_POST['username'];

      $password = $_POST['password'];

        $count=0;

        $res=mysqli_query($db,"SELECT * FROM `admin` WHERE
username='$username';")

        $row=mysqli_fetch_assoc($res);

        $count=mysqli_num_rows($res);

        if($count==0)

        {

        ?>

        <!--

        <script>

          alert("The username and password don't exist.")

        </script>

        -->
```

```php
            <div class="alert alert-danger" style="width:
700px; margin-left: 360px; background-color: rgb(132, 57,
57); color: white; border-color:rgb(8, 23, 3, 10);">

                <strong>The username and password don't
exist.</strong>


    </div>

    <?php

        }

    else{

        /*-----------------if username & password
matches----------*/

        $_SESSION['login_user'] = $_POST['username'];

        $_SESSION['pic'] = $row['pic'];

        if(password_verify($password, $row['password']))
{

        ?>

        <script>

          window.location="profile.php";

        </script>

          <?php

    }

    if(mysqli_query($db, "SELECT * FROM `admin` WHERE
username='$username' && password='$password';")) {

        ?>

        <script>

        window.location="profile.php";

        </script>

        <?php
```

```
        }

        }

        }

    ?>


</body>

</html>
```

This is how it looks:

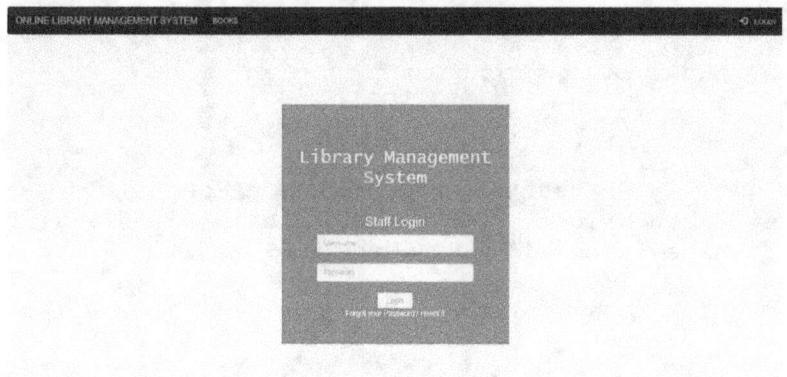

Figure 7-1: How admin_login.php

Next, this is the code for ***profile.php***.

```php
<?php

    include "connection.php";

    include "navbar.php";

?>

<!DOCTYPE html>

<html>

    <head>
```

```html
<title>Edit Profile</title>

        <meta name="viewport" content="width=device-width,
initial-scale=1.0">



<meta http-equiv="X-UA-Compatible"
content="IE=edge,chrome=1">

<meta name="HandheldFriendly" content="true">



</head>

    <body style="background-color: white;">

        <div class="container">

            <form action="" method="post">

                <button class="btn btn-default"
style="float: right; background-color: #f3f402; width:
70px;" name="submit1" type="submit">

                    Edit

                </button>

            </form>

            <div class="wrapper">

                <?php

                if(isset($_POST['submit1']))

                {

                    ?>

                        <script>

                            window.location="edit.php";

                        </script>

                    <?php
```

```php
                }
                $q=mysqli_query($db,"SELECT * FROM
admin where username='$_SESSION[login_user]' ;");
                ?>

                <h2 style="text-align: center;">Staff
Info</h2>
                <?php

    $row=mysqli_fetch_assoc($q);


if($row['login'] == "no") {

                    ?>

                    <div class="alert">

    <p>Please change your password! <a href="must.php">Click
here to change it!</a></p>

</div>

                    <?php

                }
                echo "<div style='text-align: center;'>

                <img class='img-circle profile_img'
height='110' width='120'
src='images/".$_SESSION['pic']."'>

                </div>";

            ?>
            <div style="text-align: center;">

                <strong>Welcome, </strong>

            <h4>

                <?php echo $_SESSION['login_user']; ?>

            </h4>
```

```
                    </div>


        <?php
                            echo "<b>";
                    echo "<table class='table table-
bordered'>";
                        echo "<tr>";
                            echo "<td>";
                                echo "<b>Username: </b>";
                            echo "</td>";

                            echo "<td>";
                                echo $row['username'];
                            echo "</td>";
                        echo "</tr>";
                    echo "</table>";
                    echo "</b>";
                ?>
            </div>
        </div>
    </body>
</html>
```

This is how it looks:

Figure 7-2: What profile.php does

This is the code for ***must.php***:

```php
<?php

    include "connection.php";

    include "navbar.php";

?>

<!DOCTYPE html>

<html>

    <head>

        <title>Change your password</title>

        <meta name="viewport" content="width=device-width,
initial-scale=1.0">


<meta http-equiv="X-UA-Compatible"
content="IE=edge,chrome=1">

<meta name="HandheldFriendly" content="true">

</head>
```

```
    <body style="background-color: white; color: blue;
text-align: center;">




<h2 style="text-align: center;">Change your password</h2>


        <?php


        $sql = "SELECT * FROM `admin` WHERE
username='$_SESSION[login_user]'";

        $result = mysqli_query($db,$sql) or die
(mysqli_error());


        while ($row = mysqli_fetch_assoc($result))

        {

            $username=$row['username'];

            $password=$row['password'];

        }

        ?>

        <div class="profile_info">

                <span>Welcome,</span>

                <h4><?php echo $_SESSION['login_user'];
?></h4>

        </div><br><br>

        <div>

        <form action="" method="post"
enctype="multipart/form-data">
```

```
        <label><h4><b>Password:</b></h4></label>

<center><input type="password" name="pass1" class="form-
control" placeholder="New Password"></center>


        <label><h4><b>Confirm
Password:</b></h4></label>

        <center><input type="password"
name="pass2" class="form-control" placeholder="Confirm
Password"></center>

        <div style="padding-left: 10px;"><button
class="btn btn-default" style="color: green;"
type="submit" name="save">Save Your
Password</button></div><br><br>

    </form>

  </div>

    <?php


        if(isset($_POST['save']))

        {


        $pass1=$_POST['pass1'];

        $pass2=$_POST['pass2'];


                if($pass1 != $pass2) {

                echo "<script>alert('The
passwords do not match!')</script>";
                echo
"<script>window.location='must.php'</script>";
```

```php
                }


                        if($pass1 == $pass2) {



$options = array("cost"=>4);

        $hash =
password_hash($pass1,PASSWORD_BCRYPT,$options);



        $sql1= "UPDATE `admin` SET `password`='$hash',
`login`='yes' WHERE
`username`='".$_SESSION['login_user']."';";

        if(mysqli_query($db,$sql1))

        {

            ?>

                <script>

                        alert("Your New Password was saved
successfully!");

                        window.location="profile.php";

                </script>

                <?php

            }

            }

            }

        ?>

    </body>

</html>
```

It looks like this:

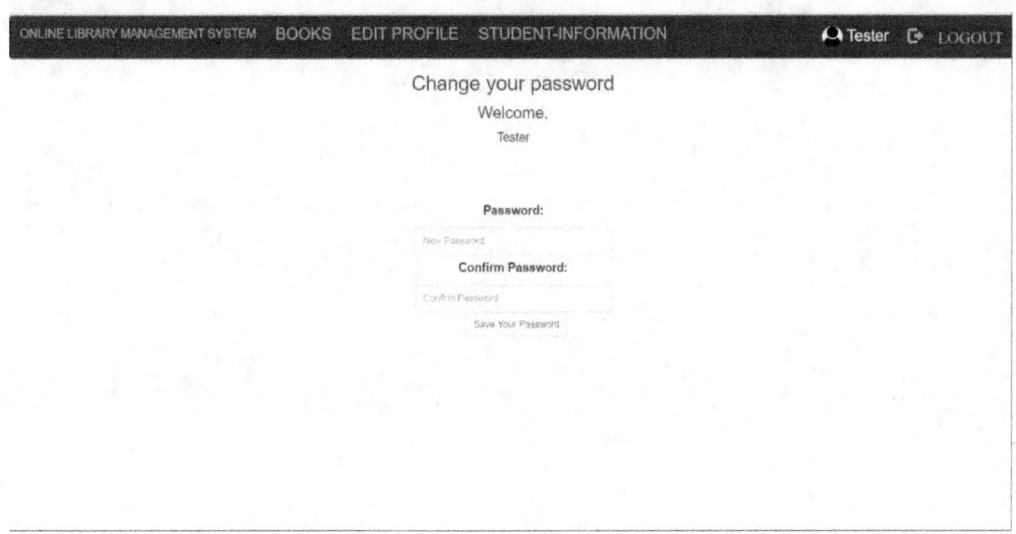

Figure 7-3: What must.php does

This is the code for *edit.php*:

```
<?php

include "connection.php";

include "navbar.php";

?>

<!DOCTYPE html>

<html>

<head>

<title>Edit Profile</title>

<meta name="viewport" content="width=device-width,
initial-scale=1.0">
```

```html
<meta http-equiv="X-UA-Compatible"
content="IE=edge,chrome=1">

<meta name="HandheldFriendly" content="true">

</head>
```

```php
<body style="background-color: white; color: blue;
text-align: center;">

        <h2 style="text-align: center;">Edit Your
Info</h2>

        <?php

        $sql = "SELECT * FROM `admin` WHERE
username='$_SESSION[login_user]'";

        $result = mysqli_query($db,$sql);

        while ($row = mysqli_fetch_assoc($result))

        {

                $username=$row['username'];

                $password=$row['password'];

        }

        ?>

        <div class="profile_info">

                <span>Welcome,</span>

                <h4><?php echo $_SESSION['login_user'];
?></h4>

        </div><br><br>

        <div>

        <form action="" method="post"
enctype="multipart/form-data">

                <center><input class="form-control"
type="file" name="file"></center>

                <label><h4><b>Username:</b></h4></label>

                <center><input disabled type="text"
name="username" class="form-control" placeholder="New
Username" value="<?php echo $username; ?>"></center>

                <label><h4><b>Password:</b></h4></label>
```

```php
            <center><input type="password"
name="password" class="form-control" placeholder="New
Password" value="<?php echo $password; ?>"></center>

                <div style="padding-left: 10px;"><button
class="btn btn-default" style="color: green;"

type="submit" name="save">Save Your
Profile</button></div><br><br>

        </form>

    </div>

        <?php

        if($rows['login'] == "yes") {


            if(isset($_POST['save']))

            {

move_uploaded_file($_FILES['file']['tmp_name'],
"images/".$_FILES['file']['name']);


                $username=$_POST['username'];

                $password=$_POST['password'];

                $pic=$_FILES['file']['name'];


                $options = array("cost"=>4);

        $hash =
password_hash($password,PASSWORD_BCRYPT,$options);

                $sql1= "UPDATE `admin` SET `pic`='$pic',
`username`='$username', `password`='$password' WHERE
`username`='".$_SESSION['login_user']."';";


                if(mysqli_query($db,$sql1))
```

```php
                {
            ?>
                <script>
                    alert("Your New Profile was saved
successfully!");
                    window.location="profile.php";
                </script>
            <?php
            }


            }
            }
        ?>
    </body>
</html>
```

This is what happens when you run it:

Figure 7-4: What happens when you run edit.php

Here is the code for *books.php*:

```php
<?php

    include "connection.php";

    include "navbar.php";

?>

<!DOCTYPE HTML>

<html>

    <head>

        <title>Books</title>

        <meta name="viewport" content="width=device-width,
initial-scale=1.0">

<meta http-equiv="X-UA-Compatible"
content="IE=edge,chrome=1">

<meta name="HandheldFriendly" content="true">

        <style>

        header {

        width: 100%;

}


section {

        width: 100%;

}

footer {

        width: 100%;

}
```

```css
nav {

        width: 100%;

}
/* Tablet Landscape */
@media screen and (max-width: 1060px) {

    body { width:67%; }

    #sidenav { width:30%; margin-left:3%;}

}
/* Tabled Portrait */
@media screen and (max-width: 768px) {

    body { width:100%; }

    #sidenav { width:100%; margin:0; border:none; }

}
html { font-size:100%; }
@media (min-width: 640px) { .srch {width: 300px;} }
@media (min-width:960px) { .srch {width: 500px;} }
@media (min-width:1100px) { .srch {width: 400px;} }
@viewport {

  width: device-width ;

  zoom: 1.0 ;

}


@-ms-viewport {

  width: device-width ;

}
```

```css
        .srch
        {
            padding-left: 1000px;
        }
        * {box-sizing: border-box;}
body {font-family: Verdana, sans-serif;}
.mySlides {display: none;}
img {vertical-align middle;}


/* Slideshow container */
.slideshow-container {
  max-width: 1000px;
  position: relative;
  margin: auto;
}
/* Caption text */
.text {
  color: #f2f2f2;
  font-size: 15px;
  padding: 8px 12px;
  position: absolute;
  bottom: 8px;
  width: 100%;
  text-align: center;
}
```

```css
/* Number text (1/3 etc) */
.numbertext {
  color: #f2f2f2;
  font-size: 12px;
  padding: 8px 12px;
  position: absolute;
  top: 0;
}
/* The dots/bullets/indicators */
.dot {
  height: 15px;
  width: 15px;
  margin: 0 2px;
  background-color: #bbb;
  border-radius: 50%;
  display: inline-block;
  transition: background-color 0.6s ease;
}


.active {
  background-color: #717171;
}


/* Fading animation */
.fade {
  -webkit-animation-name: fade;
```

```css
    -webkit-animation-duration: 1.5s;
    animation-name: fade;
    animation-duration: 1.5s;
}
@-webkit-keyframes fade {
    from {opacity: .4}
    to {opacity: 1}
}
@keyframes fade {
    from {opacity: .4}
    to {opacity: 1}
}
/* On smaller screens, decrease text size */
@media only screen and (max-width: 300px) {
    .text {font-size: 11px}
}
body {
    font-family: "Lato", sans-serif;
    transition: background-color .5s;
    margin-right: 100px;
}
.sidenav {
    height: 100%;
    margin-top: 50px;
    width: 0;
    position: fixed;
```

```
    z-index: 1;

    top: 0;

    left: 0;

    background-color: lightgreen;

    overflow-x: hidden;

    transition: 0.5s;

    padding-top: 60px;

}


.sidenav a {

    padding: 8px 8px 8px 32px;

    text-decoration: none;

    font-size: 25px;

    color: #818181;

    display: block;

    transition: 0.3s;

}
.sidenav a:hover {

    color: #f1f1f1;

}
.sidenav .closebtn {

    position: absolute;

    top: 0;

    right: 25px;

    font-size: 36px;

    margin-left: 50px;
```

```css
}

#main {

  transition: margin-left .5s;

  padding: 16px;

}

@media screen and (max-height: 450px) {

  .sidenav {padding-top: 15px;}

  .sidenav a {font-size: 18px;}

}

.img-circle

{

    margin-left: 20px;

}

.pop:hover

{

    color: white;

    width: 300px;

    height: 50px;

    background-color: blue;

}

    </style>
```

```html
<link rel="stylesheet"
href="https://maxcdn.bootstrapcdn.com/bootstrap/3.4.0/css/
bootstrap.min.css">

<script
src="https://ajax.googleapis.com/ajax/libs/jquery/3.4.0/jq
uery.min.js"></script>
```

```
<script
src="https://maxcdn.bootstrapcdn.com/bootstrap/3.4.0/js/bo
otstrap.min.js"></script>

    </head>

    <body>

        <!--
_____sidenav_____
_____-->


    <div id="mySidenav" class="sidenav" style="text-
decoration: none;">

  <a href="javascript:void(0)" class="closebtn"
onclick="closeNav()" style="text-decoration:
none;">&times;</a>



                    <div style="color: white; margin-
left: 60px; font-size: 20px;">

                    <?php

                    if(isset($_SESSION['login_user']))

                    { echo "<img class='img-circle
profile_img' height=120 width=120
src='images/".$_SESSION['pic']."'>";

                    echo "</br></br>";


                    echo "Welcome
".$_SESSION['login_user'];

                    }

                ?>

                </div><br><br>


<div class="pop">  <a href="add_student.php" style="text-
decoration: none;">Add Student</a> </div>
```

```html
<div class="pop">  <a href="issue_info.php" style="text-
decoration: none;">Issue Information</a> </div>

<div class="pop"> <a href="add_books.php" style="text-
decoration: none;">Add Books</a></div>

</div>

<div id="main">

  <span style="font-size:30px;cursor:pointer"
onclick="openNav()">&#9776; open</span>

<script>

function openNav() {

  document.getElementById("mySidenav").style.width =
"300px";

  document.getElementById("main").style.marginLeft =
"300px";

  document.body.style.backgroundColor = "rgba(0,0,0,0.4)";

}

function closeNav() {

  document.getElementById("mySidenav").style.width = "0";

  document.getElementById("main").style.marginLeft= "0";

  document.body.style.backgroundColor = "white";

}

</script>

    <!--_____search
bar_____-->


    <div class="srch">

        <form class="navbar-form" method="post"
name="form1">
```

```
            <input class="form-control" type="text"
name="search" placeholder="Search for a book..."
required="">

            <button style="background-color:
lightgreen;" type="submit" name="submit" class="btn btn-
default">

                <span class="glyphicon glyphicon-
search"></span>

            </button><br><br>

        </form>

        <form method="post" class="navbar-form"
name="form2">

                <input class="form-control"
type="text" name="bid" placeholder="Search for a Book
ID..." required="">

                <button style="background-color:
lightgreen;" type="submit" name="delete" class="btn btn-
default">Delete a Book</button><br>

        </form>

        <p class="demo"></p>

</div>

    <?php


    if(isset($_POST['submit']))

    {

        $q=mysqli_query($db,"SELECT * FROM books where
title like '%$_POST[search]%' ");


        if(mysqli_num_rows($q)==0)

        {
```

```php
        echo "Sorry, I didn't get that. Try
checking: <br> 1. Spelling <br> 2. Try another phrase <br>
3. The book does not exist";

        }

        else

        {

        echo "<table class='table table-bordered
table-hover'>";

        // Table rows(tr)

        echo "<tr style='background-color:
lightgreen;'>";

        // Table header(th)

        echo "<th>";  echo "ID";    echo "</th>";

        echo "<th>";  echo "ISBN No.";  echo "</th>";

        echo "<th>";  echo "Title";    echo "</th>";

        echo "<th>";  echo "Author(s)";    echo "</th>";

        echo "<th>";  echo "Publisher";    echo "</th>";

        echo "<th>";  echo "Status";    echo "</th>";

        echo "<th>";  echo "Quantity";  echo "</th>";

        echo "<th>";  echo "Section";  echo "</th>";

        echo "</tr>";

while($row=mysqli_fetch_assoc($q))

{

echo "<tr>";

// Table data(td)

        echo "<td>"; echo $row['bid']; echo "</td>";

        echo "<td>"; echo $row['isbn']; echo "</td>";

        echo "<td>"; echo $row['title']; echo "</td>";
```

```php
        echo "<td>"; echo $row['authors']; echo "</td>";

        echo "<td>"; echo $row['publisher']; echo "</td>";

        echo "<td>"; echo $row['status']; echo "</td>";

        echo "<td>"; echo $row['quantity']; echo "</td>";

        echo "<td>"; echo $row['section']; echo "</td>";

    echo "</tr>";

    }

    echo "</table>";

        }

    }

        /*if button is not pressed*/

        else

        {

        ?>

    <center><div class="slideshow-container">

        <h1>Favourite Books</h1><br>

<div class="mySlides fade">

    <div class="numbertext">1 / 3</div>

    <img
src="http://cdn.shopify.com/s/files/1/0028/5468/2689/produ
cts/STIM9781407106175_BK_grande.jpg?v=1530118311"
style="width: 200px; height: 200px;">

    <br><br><br>

    <div class="text" style="color: blue;">Stick Man, Julia
Donaldson &amp; Axel Scheffler, 21 August 2008</div>

</div>


<div class="mySlides fade">
```

```
<div class="numbertext">2 / 3</div>

<img src="https://images-na.ssl-images-
amazon.com/images/I/51%2BV5g3Q9WL._SX324_BO1,204,203,200_.
jpg" style="width: 200px; height: 200px;">

<br><br><br>

<div class="text" style="color: blue;">Catching Falling
Stars, Karen McCombie, 4 June 2015</div>

</div>


<div class="mySlides fade">

<div class="numbertext">3 / 3</div>

<img src="https://images-na.ssl-images-
amazon.com/images/I/61t3K7PGljL._SX258_BO1,204,203,200_.jp
g" style="width: 200px; height: 200px;">

<br><br><br>

<div class="text" style="color: blue;">Farmer Duck,
Marin Waddell &amp; Helen Oxenbury, 1991</div>

</div>


</div> </center>

<br>


<div style="text-align:center">

<span class="dot"></span>

<span class="dot"></span>

<span class="dot"></span>

</div>

<script>

var slideIndex = 0;
```

```
showSlides();

function showSlides() {

  var i;

  var slides =
document.getElementsByClassName("mySlides");

  var dots = document.getElementsByClassName("dot");

  for (i = 0; i < slides.length; i++) {

    slides[i].style.display = "none";

  }

  slideIndex++;

  if (slideIndex > slides.length) {slideIndex = 1}

  for (i = 0; i < dots.length; i++) {

    dots[i].className = dots[i].className.replace("
active", "");

  }

  slides[slideIndex-1].style.display = "block";

  dots[slideIndex-1].className += " active";

  setTimeout(showSlides, 2000); // Change image every 2
seconds

}

</script>


        <?php

        }


        if(isset($_SESSION['login_user'])) {

            if(isset($_POST['delete'])) {
```

```php
                    mysqli_query($db,"DELETE FROM books WHERE
bid='$_POST[bid]' ;");

                ?>

            <script>

                alert("The book was deleted
successfully!");

                </script>

        <?php

        }

        }

        else

        {

         ?>

         <script>

             alert("You need to login first!");

        </script>

        <?php

        }

    ?>

    </body>

</html>
```

This is what it does:

Figure 7-5: What books.php does

This is the complete code for ***student.php***:

```php
<?php

    include "connection.php";

    include "navbar.php";

?>

<!DOCTYPE HTML>

<html>

    <head>

        <title>Students</title>

        <meta name="viewport" content="width=device-width,
initial-scale=1.0">



<meta http-equiv="X-UA-Compatible"
content="IE=edge,chrome=1">

<meta name="HandheldFriendly" content="true">



        <style>
```

```css
        header {

                width: 100%;

}


section {

                width: 100%;

}


footer {

                width: 100%;

}


nav {

                width: 100%;

}


/* Tablet Landscape */
@media screen and (max-width: 1060px) {
        body { width:67%; }
        #sidenav { width:30%; margin-left:3%;}
}
/* Tabled Portrait */
@media screen and (max-width: 768px) {
        body { width:100%; }
        #sidenav { width:100%; margin:0; border:none; }
}
```

```css
html { font-size:100%; }
@media (min-width: 640px) { body {font-size:1rem;} }
@media (min-width:960px) { body {font-size:1.2rem;} }
@media (min-width:1100px) { body {font-size:1.5rem;} }
@viewport {
  width: device-width ;
  zoom: 1.0 ;
}


@-ms-viewport {
  width: device-width ;
}
        .srch
        {
            padding-left: 1000px;
        }


        * {box-sizing: border-box;}
body {font-family: Verdana, sans-serif;}
.mySlides {display: none;}
img {vertical-align middle;}

/* Slideshow container */
.slideshow-container {
  max-width: 1000px;
```

```css
    position: relative;

    margin: auto;

}

/* Caption text */

.text {

    color: #f2f2f2;

    font-size: 15px;

    padding: 8px 12px;

    position: absolute;

    bottom: 8px;

    width: 100%;

    text-align: center;

}


/* Number text (1/3 etc) */

.numbertext {

    color: #f2f2f2;

    font-size: 12px;

    padding: 8px 12px;

    position: absolute;

    top: 0;

}


/* The dots/bullets/indicators */

.dot {

    height: 15px;
```

```css
  width: 15px;

  margin: 0 2px;

  background-color: #bbb;

  border-radius: 50%;

  display: inline-block;

  transition: background-color 0.6s ease;

}


.active {

  background-color: #717171;

}


/* Fading animation */
.fade {

  -webkit-animation-name: fade;

  -webkit-animation-duration: 1.5s;

  animation-name: fade;

  animation-duration: 1.5s;

}


@-webkit-keyframes fade {

  from {opacity: .4}

  to {opacity: 1}

}


@keyframes fade {
```

```css
  from {opacity: .4}
  to {opacity: 1}
}


/* On smaller screens, decrease text size */
@media only screen and (max-width: 300px) {
  .text {font-size: 11px}
}


body {
  font-family: "Lato", sans-serif;
  transition: background-color .5s;
  margin-right: 100px;
}


.sidenav {
  height: 100%;
  margin-top: 50px;
  width: 0;
  position: fixed;
  z-index: 1;
  top: 0;
  left: 0;
  background-color: lightgreen;
  overflow-x: hidden;
  transition: 0.5s;
```

```css
  padding-top: 60px;
}


.sidenav a {
  padding: 8px 8px 8px 32px;
  text-decoration: none;
  font-size: 25px;
  color: #818181;
  display: block;
  transition: 0.3s;
}


.sidenav a:hover {
  color: #f1f1f1;
}


.sidenav .closebtn {
  position: absolute;
  top: 0;
  right: 25px;
  font-size: 36px;
  margin-left: 50px;
}


#main {
  transition: margin-left .5s;
```

```css
    padding: 16px;

}


@media screen and (max-height: 450px) {

  .sidenav {padding-top: 15px;}

  .sidenav a {font-size: 18px;}

}

.img-circle

{

    margin-left: 20px;

}


.pop:hover

{

    color: white;

    width: 300px;

    height: 50px;

    background-color: blue;

}

        </style>


<link rel="stylesheet"
href="https://maxcdn.bootstrapcdn.com/bootstrap/3.4.0/css/
bootstrap.min.css">

<script
src="https://ajax.googleapis.com/ajax/libs/jquery/3.4.0/jq
uery.min.js"></script>
```

```
<script
src="https://maxcdn.bootstrapcdn.com/bootstrap/3.4.0/js/bo
otstrap.min.js"></script>

    </head>

    <body>

        <!--
_____sidenav_____
_____-->


    <div id="mySidenav" class="sidenav" style="text-
decoration: none;">

  <a href="javascript:void(0)" class="closebtn"
onclick="closeNav()" style="text-decoration:
none;">&times;</a>



                    <div style="color: white; margin-
left: 60px; font-size: 20px;">

                    <?php

                    if(isset($_SESSION['login_user']))

                    { echo "<img class='img-circle
profile_img' height=120 width=120
src='images/".$_SESSION['pic']."'>";

                    echo "</br></br>";



                    echo "Welcome
".$_SESSION['login_user'];

                    }

                    ?>

                    </div><br><br>


<div class="pop">  <a href="add_student.php" style="text-
decoration: none;">Add Students </a> </div>
```

```
<div class="pop">  <a href="issue_info.php" style="text-
decoration: none;">Issue Information</a> </div>

<div class="pop"> <a href="expired.php" style="text-
decoration: none;">Expired Books List</a></div>

</div>


<div id="main">

  <span style="font-size:30px;cursor:pointer"
onclick="openNav()">&#9776; open</span>


<script>

function openNav() {

  document.getElementById("mySidenav").style.width =
"300px";

  document.getElementById("main").style.marginLeft =
"300px";

  document.body.style.backgroundColor = "rgba(0,0,0,0.4)";

}

function closeNav() {

  document.getElementById("mySidenav").style.width = "0";

  document.getElementById("main").style.marginLeft= "0";

  document.body.style.backgroundColor = "white";

}

</script>

     <!--_____search
bar_____-->


     <div class="srch">
```

```html
<form class="navbar-form" method="post"
name="form1">

            <input class="form-control" type="text"
name="search" placeholder="Search for a student..."
required="">

            <button style="background-color:
lightgreen;" type="submit" name="submit" class="btn btn-
default">

                <span class="glyphicon glyphicon-
search"></span>

            </button><br><br>

    </form>

    <form method="post" class="navbar-form"
name="form2">

            <input class="form-control"
type="text" name="bid" placeholder="Search for a
username..." required="">

            <button style="background-color:
lightgreen;" type="submit" name="delete" class="btn btn-
default">Delete a Student</button><br>

    </form>

</div>
```

```php
    <?php

    if(isset($_POST['submit']))

    {

        $q=mysqli_query($db,"SELECT * FROM student
WHERE username LIKE '%$_POST[search]%' ");


        $res=mysqli_query($db,"SELECT
first,last,username,id,contact FROM student");


        if(mysqli_num_rows($q)==0)
```

```
                {
                        echo "Sorry, I didn't get that. Try
checking: <br> 1. Spelling <br> 2. Try another phrase <br>
3. The student does not exist";

                }
                else

                {
                        echo "<table class='table table-bordered
table-hover'>";

                        // Table rows(tr)
                        echo "<tr style='background-color:
lightgreen;'>";

                        // Table header(th)
                        echo "<th>";  echo "First Name";  echo "</th>";

                        echo "<th>";  echo "Last Name";   echo "</th>";

                        echo "<th>";  echo "Username";    echo "</th>";

                        echo "<th>";  echo "Password";    echo "</th>";

                        echo "<th>";  echo "Class";    echo "</th>";

                        echo "<th>";  echo "Library ID";    echo "</th>";


                        echo "</tr>";


        while($row=mysqli_fetch_assoc($q))

        {

        echo "<tr>";

        // Table data(td)
                echo "<td>"; echo $row['first']; echo "</td>";

                echo "<td>"; echo $row['last']; echo "</td>";
```

```php
        echo "<td>"; echo $row['username']; echo "</td>";

        echo "<td>"; echo $row['password']; echo "</td>";

        echo "<td>"; echo $row['class']; echo "</td>";

        echo "<td>"; echo $row['id']; echo "</td>";


    echo "</tr>";

    }

  echo "</table>";

        }


    }


    if(isset($_POST['delete']))

    {

        if(isset($_SESSION['login_user']))

        {

            mysqli_query($db,"DELETE FROM student WHERE
username='$_POST[username]' ;");

            ?>

                <script>

                    alert("The student was deleted
successfully!");

                </script>

        <?php

        }

        else

        {
```

```
        ?>
        <script>
            alert("You need to login first!");
        </script>
        <?php
    }
}


    ?>
    </body>
</html>
```

What happens when you run **student.php**:

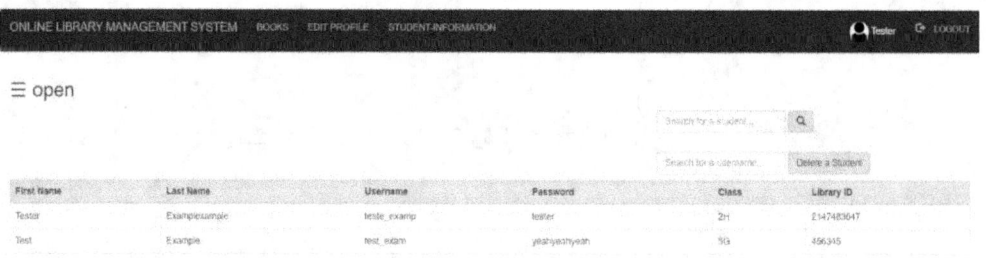

Figure 7-6: What student.php does

This is the code for **issue_book.php**:

```php
<?php
    include "connection.php";
    include "navbar.php";
```

```
?>

<!DOCTYPE html>

<html>

<head>

    <title>Borrow Information</title>

    <meta name="viewport" content="width=device-width,
initial-scale=1.0">


<meta http-equiv="X-UA-Compatible"
content="IE=edge,chrome=1">

<meta name="HandheldFriendly" content="true">


    <style type="text/css">


.srch

        {

            padding-left: 850px;


        }

        .form-control

        {

            width: 300px;

            height: 40px;

            background-color: white;

            color: black;

        }
```

```css
body {

        background-image: url("images/open.png");

    font-family: "Lato", sans-serif;

    transition: background-color .5s;

}


.sidenav {

    height: 100%;

    margin-top: 50px;

    width: 0;

    position: fixed;

    z-index: 1;

    top: 0;

    left: 0;

    background-color: lightgreen;

    overflow-x: hidden;

    transition: 0.5s;

    padding-top: 60px;

}


.sidenav a {

    padding: 8px 8px 8px 32px;

    text-decoration: none;

    font-size: 25px;

    color: #818181;

    display: block;
```

```css
    transition: 0.3s;

}


.sidenav a:hover {

    color: white;

}


.sidenav .closebtn {

    position: absolute;

    top: 0;

    right: 25px;

    font-size: 36px;

    margin-left: 50px;

}


#main {

    transition: margin-left .5s;

    padding: 16px;

}


@media screen and (max-height: 450px) {

    .sidenav {padding-top: 15px;}

    .sidenav a {font-size: 18px;}

}

.img-circle

{
```

```css
        margin-left: 20px;
}
.h:hover
{
    color: black;
    width: 300px;
    height: 50px;
    background-color: blue;
}
.container
{
    height: 750px;
    background-color: white;
    opacity: .8;
    color: black;
}


.scroll
{
    width: 100%;
    height: 500px;
    overflow: auto;
}


    </style>
```

```
</head>

<body>

<!--_____sidenav_____-->


    <div id="mySidenav" class="sidenav">

  <a href="javascript:void(0)" class="closebtn"
onclick="closeNav()">&times;</a>



            <div style="color: white; margin-left: 60px;
font-size: 20px;">



            <?php

            if(isset($_SESSION['login_user']))



            { echo "<img class='img-circle
profile_img' height=120 width=120
src='images/".$_SESSION['pic']."'>";

            echo "</br></br>";



            echo "Welcome
".$_SESSION['login_user'];

            }

            ?>

        </div><br><br>


  <div class="h"> <a href="books.php">Books</a></div>

  <div class="h"> <a href="issue_info.php">Issue
Information</a></div>
```

```
<div class="h"> <a href="expired.php">Expired Books
List</a></div>

</div>

<div id="main">

  <span style="font-size:30px;cursor:pointer"
onclick="openNav()">&#9776; open</span>


    <script>

    function openNav() {

        document.getElementById("mySidenav").style.width =
"300px";

        document.getElementById("main").style.marginLeft =
"300px";

        document.body.style.backgroundColor =
"rgba(0,0,0,0.4)";

        }


    function closeNav() {

        document.getElementById("mySidenav").style.width =
"0";

        document.getElementById("main").style.marginLeft=
"0";

        document.body.style.backgroundColor = "white";

        }

    </script>


    <br><br>


    <div class="container">
```

```php
        <h3 style="text-align: center; font-weight:
bold;">Information of Borrowed Books</h3>



        <?php

        $c=0;



            if(isset($_SESSION['login_user']))

                {

                $sql="SELECT
student.username,id,books.bid,books.isbn,title,authors,pub
lisher,borrow_date,return_date FROM student inner join
issue_book ON student.username=issue_book.username inner
join books ON issue_book.bid=books.bid WHERE
issue_book.approve ='Borrowed' ORDER BY
`issue_book`.`return_date` ASC";

                $res=mysqli_query($db,$sql);



                echo "<div class='scroll'>";



                echo "<table class='table table-bordered'
style='width: 100%;'>";

                echo "<tr style='background-color: black;
color: white;'>";

                //Table header



                    echo "<th>"; echo "Username";  echo
"</th>";

                    echo "<th>"; echo "Library ID";  echo
"</th>";

                    echo "<th>"; echo "Book ID";  echo
"</th>";
```

```php
                              echo "<th>"; echo "ISBN
No."; echo "</th>";

                    echo "<th>"; echo "Book Title";  echo
"</th>";

                    echo "<th>"; echo "Authors";  echo
"</th>";

                    echo "<th>"; echo "Publisher";  echo
"</th>";

                         echo "<th>"; echo "Borrow
Date"; echo "</th>";

                         echo "<th>"; echo "Return
Date";  echo "</th>";


          echo "</tr>";


          while($row=mysqli_fetch_assoc($res))

          {

             $d=date("Y-m-d");

             if($d > $row['return_date'])

             {

                  $c=$c+1;

                  $var='<p style="color: yellow;
background-color: red;">EXPIRED</p>';


                  mysqli_query($db,"UPDATE issue_book
SET approve='$var' WHERE `return_date`='$row[return_date]'
and approve='Yes' LIMIT $c;");


                  echo $d."</br>";

          }
```

```php
                    echo "<tr>";
                    echo "<td>"; echo $row['username']; echo
"</td>";

                    echo "<td>"; echo $row['id']; echo
"</td>";

                    echo "<td>"; echo $row['bid']; echo
"</td>";

                                    echo "<td>"; echo
$row['isbn']; echo "</td>";

                    echo "<td>"; echo $row['title']; echo
"</td>";

                    echo "<td>"; echo $row['authors']; echo
"</td>";

                    echo "<td>"; echo $row['publisher'];
echo "</td>";

                                    echo "<td>"; echo
$row['borrow_date']; echo "</td>";

                                echo "<td>"; echo
$row['return_date']; echo "</td>";


                    echo "</tr>";
            }
        echo "</table>";
        echo "</div>";


            }


            else

            {
```

```php
                    ?>

                    <h3 style="text-align: center; font-
weight: bold;">You MUST login before you can see the
information of borrowed books</h3>

                    <?php

            }

        ?>

    </div>

</div>

</body>

</html>
```

This is what it does:

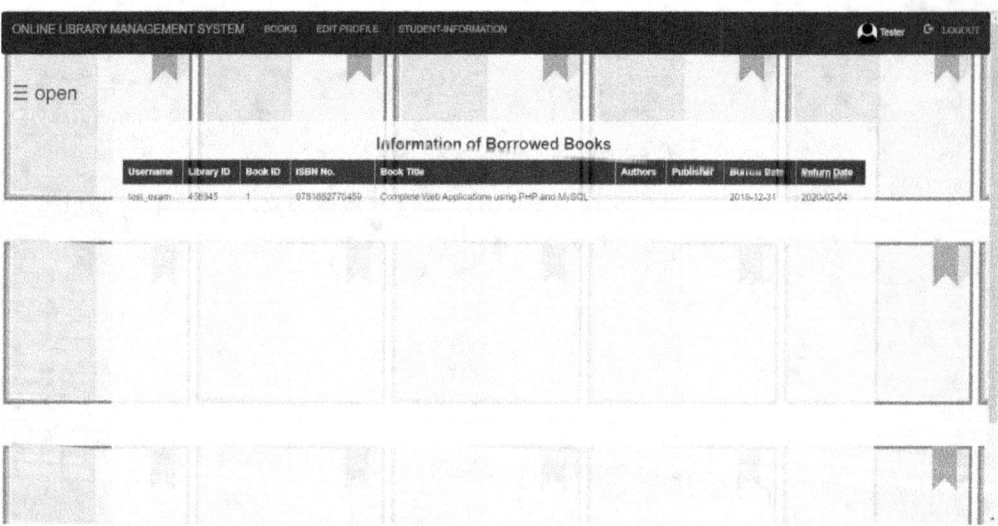

Figure 7-7: What issue_book.php looks like

This is the complete code for *logout.php*:

```php
<?php

    session_start();

    if(isset($_SESSION['login_user']))
```

```php
    {
        unset($_SESSION['login_user']);
    }
    header("location:admin_login.php");
?>
```

Here is the complete code for *forgot.php*:

```php
<?php
    include "connection.php";
    include "navbar.php";
?>
<!DOCTYPE html>
<html>
<head>
    <title>Change Password</title>
        <meta name="viewport" content="width=device-width,initial-scale=1,maximum-scale=1,user-scalable=no">


<meta http-equiv="X-UA-Compatible" content="IE=edge,chrome=1">

<meta name="HandheldFriendly" content="true">


    <style type="text/css">
        header {
        width: 100%;
}

section {
```

```
        width: 100%;

}


footer {

        width: 100%;

}


nav {

        width: 100%;

}


/* Tablet Landscape */
@media screen and (max-width: 1060px) {

    body { width:67%; }

    #sidenav { width:30%; margin-left:3%;}

}
/* Tabled Portrait */
@media screen and (max-width: 768px) {

    body { width:100%; }

    #sidenav { width:100%; margin:0; border:none; }

}


html { font-size:100%; }
@media (min-width: 640px) { body {font-size:1rem;} }
@media (min-width:960px) { body {font-size:1.2rem;} }
@media (min-width:1100px) { body {font-size:1.5rem;} }
```

```css
@viewport {

  width: device-width ;

  zoom: 1.0 ;

}


@-ms-viewport {

  width: device-width ;

}
        body
        {
            height: 650px;

            background-image: url("images/7.jpg");

            background-repeat: no-repeat;

        }
        .wrapper
        {
            width: 400px;

            height: 400px;

            margin:100px auto;

            background-color: black;

            opacity: .8;

            color: white;

            padding: 27px 15px;

        }
        .form-control
```

```
            {

                    width: 300px;

            }

    </style>

</head>

<body>

    <div class="wrapper">

        <div style="text-align: center;">

                <h1 style="text-align: center; font-size:
35px;font-family: Lucida Console;">Change Your
Password</h1>

        </div>

        <div style="padding-left: 30px; ">

        <form action="" method="post" >

                <input type="text" name="username"
class="form-control" placeholder="Username"
required=""><br>

                <input type="email" name="email" class="form-
control" placeholder="Email" required=""><br>

                <input type="password" name="password"
class="form-control" placeholder="New Password (Write it
down!)" required=""><br>

                <button class="btn btn-default" type="submit"
name="submit" >Update</button>

        </form>


    </div>


    <?php
```

```php
        if(isset($_POST['submit']))

        {

                $options = array("cost"=>4);

        $hash =
password_hash($_POST['password'],PASSWORD_BCRYPT,$options)
;

                if(mysqli_query($db,"UPDATE admin SET
password='$hash' WHERE username='$_POST[username]'

                AND email='$_POST[email]' ;"))

                {

                    ?>

                        <script type="text/javascript">

                    alert("The Password Updated
Successfully.");

                    </script>


                    <?php

                }

        }

    ?></div>
</body>
</html>
```

This is what it does:

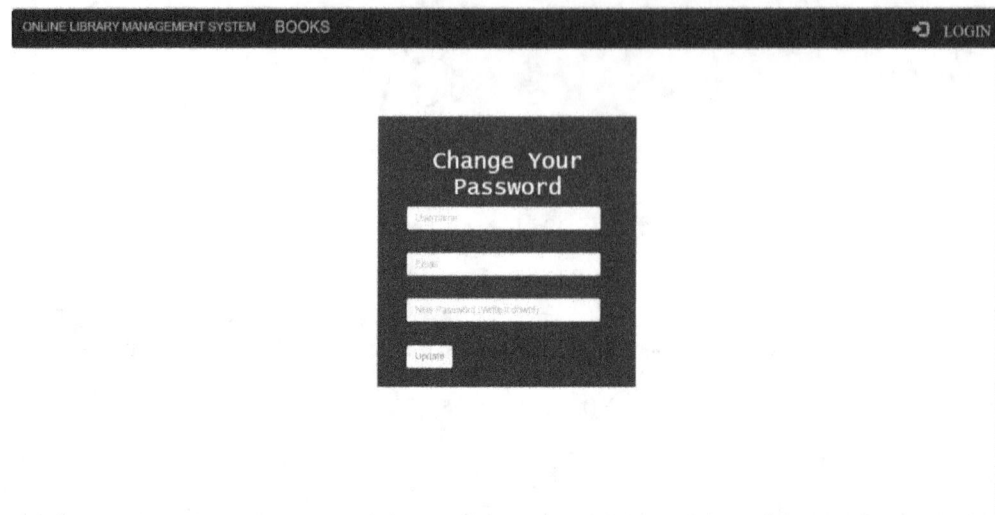

Figure 7-8: What forgot.php does

Here is the code for *expired.php*:

```php
<?php

    include "connection.php";

    include "navbar.php";

?>

<!DOCTYPE html>

<html>

<head>

    <title>Book Request</title>

    <meta name="viewport" content="width=device-width,
initial-scale=1">


    <style type="text/css">
```

```css
.srch

{

        padding-left: 70%;


}
.form-control

{

        width: 300px;

        height: 40px;

        background-color: white;

        color: black;

}

body {

        background-image: url("images/open.jpg");

        background-repeat: no-repeat;

    font-family: "Lato", sans-serif;

    transition: background-color .5s;

}


.sidenav {

  height: 100%;

  margin-top: 50px;

  width: 0;

  position: fixed;

  z-index: 1;
```

```css
    top: 0;

    left: 0;

    background-color: lightgreen;

    overflow-x: hidden;

    transition: 0.5s;

    padding-top: 60px;
}


.sidenav a {

    padding: 8px 8px 8px 32px;

    text-decoration: none;

    font-size: 25px;

    color: #818181;

    display: block;

    transition: 0.3s;
}


.sidenav a:hover {

    color: white;
}


.sidenav .closebtn {

    position: absolute;

    top: 0;

    right: 25px;

    font-size: 36px;
```

```css
    margin-left: 50px;

}


#main {

  transition: margin-left .5s;

  padding-left: 15px;

}


@media screen and (max-height: 450px) {

  .sidenav {padding-top: 15px;}

  .sidenav a {font-size: 18px;}

}
.img-circle

{

    margin-left: 20px;

}
.h:hover

{

    color:white;

    width: 300px;

    height: 50px;

    background-color: blue;

}
.container

{

    height: 800px;
```

```css
    width: 85%;

    background-color: white;

    opacity: .8;

    color: black;

  margin-top: -65px;

}

.scroll

{

  width: 100%;

  height: 400px;

  overflow: auto;

}

th,td

{

  width: 10%;

}


    </style>
```

```html
</head>
<body>
<!--_____sidenav_____-->


    <div id="mySidenav" class="sidenav">

    <a href="javascript:void(0)" class="closebtn"
onclick="closeNav()">&times;</a>
```

```
            <div style="color: white; margin-left: 60px;
font-size: 20px;">



            <?php

            if(isset($_SESSION['login_user']))



            { echo "<img class='img-circle
profile_img' height=120 width=120
src='images/".$_SESSION['pic']."'>";

            echo "</br></br>";



            echo "Welcome
".$_SESSION['login_user'];

            }

            ?>

        </div><br><br>


  <div class="h"> <a href="books.php">Books</a></div>

  <div class="h"> <a href="issue_info.php">Issue
Information</a></div>

  <div class="h"><a href="expired.php">Expired Books
List</a></div>

</div>

<div id="main">

  <span style="font-size:30px;cursor:pointer"
onclick="openNav()">&#9776; open</span>

    <script>

    function openNav() {
```

```
        document.getElementById("mySidenav").style.width =
"300px";

        document.getElementById("main").style.marginLeft =
"300px";

        document.body.style.backgroundColor =
"rgba(0,0,0,0.4)";

    }


    function closeNav() {

        document.getElementById("mySidenav").style.width =
"0";

        document.getElementById("main").style.marginLeft=
"0";

        document.body.style.backgroundColor = "white";

    }
    </script>
  <div class="container">


    <?php
      if(isset($_SESSION['login_user']))

      {

        ?>


          <div class="srch" >

          <br>

          <form method="post" action="" name="form1">

              <input type="text" name="username"
class="form-control" placeholder="Username"
required=""><br>
```

```php
        <input type="text" name="bid" class="form-
control" placeholder="Book ID" required=""><br>

        <button class="btn btn-default" name="submit"
type="submit">Submit</button><br><br>

    </form>

</div>

<?php


if(isset($_POST['submit']))

{

    $var1='<p style="color:yellow; background-
color:green;">RETURNED</p>';

    mysqli_query($db,"UPDATE issue_book SET
approve='$var1' where username='$_POST[username]' and
bid='$_POST[bid]' ");



 mysqli_query($db,"UPDATE books SET status='Available' AND
quantity = quantity+1 WHERE bid='$_POST[bid]' ");

    }

  }


    $c=0;

    $ret='<p style="color: yellow; background-color:
green;">RETURNED</p>';

    $exp='<p style="color: yellow; background-color:
red;">EXPIRED</p>';

    $sql3="SELECT
student.username,id,books.bid,title,authors,publisher,appr
ove,borrow_date,return_date FROM student inner join
issue_book ON student.username=issue_book.username inner
join books ON issue_book.bid=books.bid WHERE
issue_book.approve ='$exp' and issue_book.approve ='$ret'
ORDER BY `issue_book`.`return_date` DESC";
```

```php
$res3=mysqli_query($db,$sql3);

echo "<table class='table table-bordered' style='width:100%;' >";

//Table header


echo "<tr style='background-color: lightgreen;'>";
echo "<th>"; echo "Username";  echo "</th>";
echo "<th>"; echo "Library ID";  echo "</th>";
echo "<th>"; echo "Book ID";  echo "</th>";
echo "<th>"; echo "Book Title";  echo "</th>";
echo "<th>"; echo "Authors";  echo "</th>";
echo "<th>"; echo "Publisher";  echo "</th>";
echo "<th>"; echo "Status";  echo "</th>";
echo "<th>"; echo "Issue Date";  echo "</th>";
echo "<th>"; echo "Return Date";  echo "</th>";
echo "</tr>";
echo "</table>";
echo "<div class='scroll'>";
echo "<table class='table table-bordered' >";
while($row=mysqli_fetch_assoc($res3))
{
echo "<tr>";
    echo "<td>"; echo $row['username']; echo "</td>";
    echo "<td>"; echo $row['id']; echo "</td>";
    echo "<td>"; echo $row['bid']; echo "</td>";
    echo "<td>"; echo $row['title']; echo "</td>";
```

```
        echo "<td>"; echo $row['authors']; echo "</td>";
        echo "<td>"; echo $row['publisher']; echo
"</td>";
        echo "<td>"; echo $row['approve']; echo "</td>";
        echo "<td>"; echo $row['borrow_date']; echo
"</td>";
        echo "<td>"; echo $row['return_date']; echo
"</td>";

    echo "</tr>";

    }

  echo "</table>";

    echo "</div>";


    ?>
  </div>
</div>
</body>
</html>
```

This is what it does:

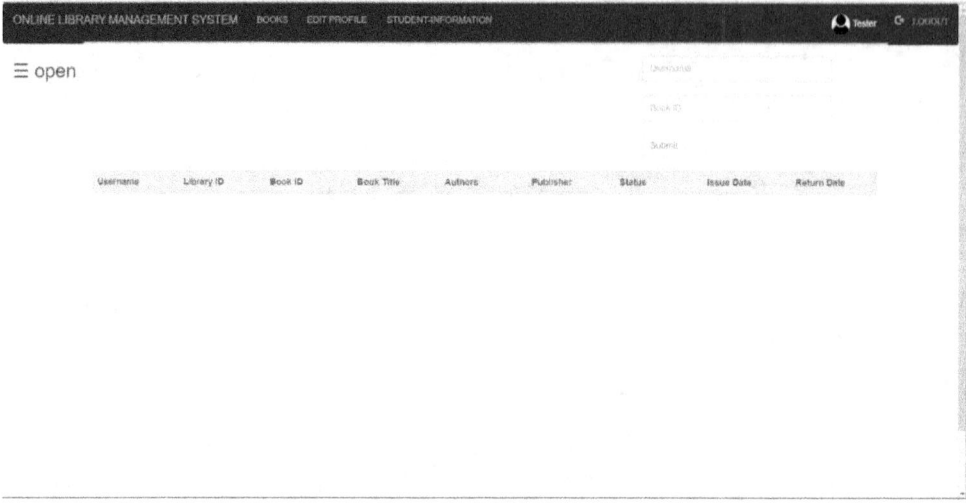

Figure 7-9: The expired.php page

This is the code for ***add_books.php***:

```php
<?php

    include "connection.php";

    include "navbar.php";

?>

<!DOCTYPE html>

<html>

    <head>

        <title>Add Books</title>

        <meta name="viewport" content="width=device-width,
initial-scale=1.0">


<meta http-equiv="X-UA-Compatible"
content="IE=edge,chrome=1">

<meta name="HandheldFriendly" content="true">


        <style>
```

```css
        header {
                width: 100%;

        }


section {
                width: 100%;

        }


footer {
                width: 100%;

        }


nav {
                width: 100%;

        }


/* Tablet Landscape */
@media screen and (max-width: 1060px) {
        body { width:67%; }
        #sidenav { width:30%; margin-left:3%; }
}
/* Tabled Portrait */
@media screen and (max-width: 768px) {
        body { width:100%; }
        #sidenav { width:100%; margin:0; border:none; }
}
```

```css
html { font-size:100%; }

@media (min-width: 640px) { body {font-size:1rem;} }

@media (min-width:960px) { body {font-size:1.2rem;} }

@media (min-width:1100px) { body {font-size:1.5rem;} }


@viewport {

  width: device-width ;

  zoom: 1.0 ;

}


@-ms-viewport {

  width: device-width ;

}
        .form-control

        {

                width: 300px;

                height: 40px;

                background-color: black;

                color: white;

        }

        </style>

    </head>

    <body style="background-color: white;">

        <h2 style="text-align: center;">Add Books</h2>

        <div>

        <form action="" method="post"
enctype="multipart/form-data">
```

```html
			<label style="text-align:
center;"><center>Front Cover Image Upload</center></label>

			<center><input class="form-control"
type="file" name="file"></center><br>


			<center><input type="text" name="isbn"
class="form-control" placeholder="ISBN No."></center><br>


			<center><input type="text" name="title"
class="form-control" placeholder="Book
Title"></center><br>


			<center><input type="text" name="authors"
class="form-control" placeholder="Book
Authors"></center><br>


			<center><input type="text"
name="publisher" class="form-control" placeholder="Book
Publisher"></center><br>


			<center><input type="text" name="status"
class="form-control" placeholder="Status"></center><br>


			<center><input type="text" name="quantity"
class="form-control" placeholder="Quantity"></center><br>


			<center><input type="text" name="section"
class="form-control" placeholder="Section"></center><br>


			<center><textarea type="text"
name="description" class="form-control"
placeholder="Description"></textarea></center><br>
```

```php
            <div style="padding-left:
10px;"><center><button class="btn btn-default"
style="color: green;" type="submit" name="add">Add
Books</button></center></div><br><br>

        </form>

    </div>

        <?php

        if(isset($_SESSION['login_user'])){


            if(isset($_POST['add']))

            {


move_uploaded_file($_FILES['file']['tmp_name'],
"images/".$_FILES['file']['name']);

        $isbn=$_POST['isbn'];

        $title=$_POST['title'];

            $authors=$_POST['authors'];

            $publisher=$_POST['publisher'];

            $status=$_POST['status'];

            $quantity=$_POST['quantity'];

            $section=$_POST['section'];

            $description=mysqli_real_escape_string($db,
$_POST['description']);

            $image=$_FILES['file']['name'];


            $sql1= "INSERT INTO books (`isbn`, `title`,
`authors`, `publisher`, `status`, `quantity`, `section`,
`description`, `image`) VALUES ('$isbn', '$title',
'$authors', '$publisher', '$status', '$quantity',
'$section', '$description', '$image');";
```

```php
            if(mysqli_query($db,$sql1) or
die(mysqli_error($db)))
            {
        ?>
                <script>
                    alert("Book added successfully!");
                </script>
            <?php
        }


        }
        }


    ?>


    </body>
</html>
```

This is how it looks:

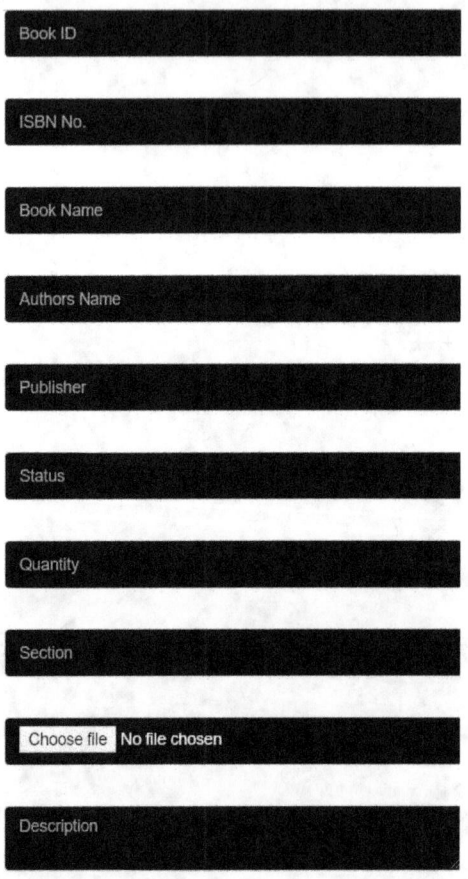

Figure 7-10: The add_books.php file

Finally, here is the code for ***add_student.php***:

```php
<?php
   include "connection.php";
   include "navbar.php";
?>


<!DOCTYPE html>
<html>
```

```
<head>

    <title>Student Registration</title>

    <link rel="stylesheet" type="text/css" href="style.css">

    <meta charset="utf-8">

    <meta name="viewport" content="width=device-width,
initial-scale=1.0">

<meta http-equiv="X-UA-Compatible"
content="IE=edge,chrome=1">

<meta name="HandheldFriendly" content="true">

    <link rel="stylesheet"
href="https://maxcdn.bootstrapcdn.com/bootstrap/3.3.7/css/
bootstrap.min.css">

    <script
src="https://ajax.googleapis.com/ajax/libs/jquery/3.3.1/jq
uery.min.js"></script>

    <script
src="https://maxcdn.bootstrapcdn.com/bootstrap/3.3.7/js/bo
otstrap.min.js"></script>

    <style type="text/css">

    header {

        width: 100%;

}


section {

        width: 100%;

}


footer {

        width: 100%;

}
```

```css
nav {

        width: 100%;

}
/* Tablet Landscape */
@media screen and (max-width: 1060px) {

    body { width:67%; }

    #sidenav { width:30%; margin-left:3%; }

}
/* Tabled Portrait */
@media screen and (max-width: 768px) {

    body { width:100%; }

    #sidenav { width:100%; margin:0; border:none; }

}


html { font-size:100%; }
@media (min-width: 640px) { body {font-size:1rem;} }
@media (min-width:960px) { body {font-size:1.2rem;} }
@media (min-width:1100px) { body {font-size:1.5rem;} }


@viewport {
  width: device-width ;
  zoom: 1.0 ;
}


@-ms-viewport {
  width: device-width ;
```

```
        }

    section

    {

      margin-top: -20px;

    }


    .form-control {

            width: 400px;

    }

  </style>

</head>

<body>


<section>

  <div class="reg_img">


    <div class="box2">

        <h1 style="text-align: center; font-size:
35px;font-family: Lucida Console;">      
Library Management System</h1>

        <h1 style="text-align: center; font-size:
25px;">Add a Student Form</h1>


    <form name="Registration" action="" method="post">


        <div class="login">

        <center>
```

```html
            <input style="width: 400px;" class="form-
control" type="text" name="first" placeholder="First Name"
required=""> <br>

            <input style="width: 400px;" class="form-
control" type="text" name="last" placeholder="Last Name"
required=""> <br>

            <input style="width: 400px;" class="form-
control" type="text" name="class" placeholder="Class"
required=""><br>

            <input style="width: 400px;" class="form-
control" type="text" name="username"
placeholder="Username" required=""> <br>

            <input style="width: 400px;" class="form-
control" type="password" name="password"
placeholder="Password" required=""> <br>

            <input style="width: 400px;" max-length="6"
class="form-control" type="text" name="id"
placeholder="Library ID - Numbers only" required=""><br>


            <input class="btn btn-default" type="submit"
name="submit" value="ADD STUDENT" style="color: black;
width: 120px; height: 30px"> </div>

    </form>

  </center>

  </div>

  </div>

</section>


  <?php


  if(isset($_POST['submit']))

  {

    $count=0;
```

```php
$sql="SELECT `username` FROM `student`";

$res=mysqli_query($db,$sql);


while($row=mysqli_fetch_assoc($res))

{

  if($row['username']==$_POST['username'])

  {

    $count=$count+1;

  }

}

if($count==0)

{

  $first = $_POST['first'];

  $last = $_POST['last'];

  $class = $_POST['class'];

  $username = $_POST['username'];

  $password = $_POST['password'];

  $id = $_POST['id'];


  mysqli_query($db,"INSERT INTO `student`
VALUES('', '$first', '$last', '$class', '$username',
'$password', '$id', 'profile.png');");

  ?>

    <script type="text/javascript">

     alert("Student registration successfully.");

    </script>

  <?php

  }
```

```php
            else
            {

              ?>

                <script type="text/javascript">
                  alert("The username already exists.");
                </script>
              <?php


            }


        }


      ?>


  </body>
  </html>
```

Library Management System

Add a Student Form

First Name

Last Name

Class

Username

Password

Library ID - Numbers only

ADD STUDENT

F

igure 7-11: How add_student.php looks like

Student Section

This is the code for *index.php*:

```php
<?php

    session_start();

?>

<!DOCTYPE html>

<html>

    <head>

        <title>

            School Library Management System

        </title>

        <meta charset="utf-8">

        <meta name="viewport" content="width=device-width,
initial-scale=1">

<style>
```

```css
/*------------------------------Main Code   INDEX -------
-------------------------------------------------*/


nav

{

  float: right;

  word-spacing: 30px;

  padding-top: 40px;

}

nav li

{

   display: inline-block;

   line-height: 60px;

}


.wrapper

{

   height: 100%;

   width: 100%;

   background-color: red;

}

header

{

     height: 150px;

     width: 100%;

     background-color: black;
```

```css
    }
    section
    {
        height: 500px;
        width: 100%;
        background-color: white;
    }
    footer
    {
        width: 100%;
        height: 200px;
        background-color: black;
    }
    .logo
    {
        float: left;
        padding-left: 20px;


    }


    li a
    {
        color: white;
        text-decoration: none;


    }
```

```css
section .sec_img
{
    height: 0px;
    width: 100%;
    margin-top: 0px;
}
.box
{

    height: 300px;
    width: 450px;
    background-color: green;
    margin: 70px auto;
    opacity: .8;
    color: blue;
}


.box {
  width: 450px;
  height: 300px;
  background-color: green;
  color: blue;
  position: relative;
   -webkit-animation: myfirst 5s linear 2s infinite
alternate; /* Safari 4.0 - 8.0 */
  animation: myfirst 5s linear 2s infinite alternate;
```

```css
}


/* Safari 4.0 - 8.0 */

@-webkit-keyframes myfirst {

    0%   {background-color:red; left:0px; top:0px;}

    25%  {background-color:yellow; left:200px; top:0px;}

    50%  {background-color:pink; left:200px; top:200px;}

    75%  {background-color:green; left:0px; top:200px;}

    100% {background-color:red; left:0px; top:0px;}

}


/* Standard syntax */

@keyframes myfirst {

    0%   {background-color:red; left:0px; top:0px;}

    25%  {background-color:yellow; left:200px; top:0px;}

    50%  {background-color:pink; left:200px; top:200px;}

    75%  {background-color:green; left:0px; top:200px;}

    100% {background-color:red; left:0px; top:0px;}

}


.glow {

    font-size: 15px;

    color: #fff;

    text-align: center;

    -webkit-animation: glow 1s ease-in-out infinite
alternate;
```

```css
  -moz-animation: glow 1s ease-in-out infinite alternate;

  animation: glow 1s ease-in-out infinite alternate;

}


@-webkit-keyframes glow {

  from {

    text-shadow: 0 0 10px #fff, 0 0 20px #fff, 0 0 30px
#00e600, 0 0 40px #00e600, 0 0 50px #00e600, 0 0 60px
#00e600, 0 0 70px #00e600;

  }


  to {

    text-shadow: 0 0 20px #fff, 0 0 30px #fff, 0 0 40px
#ff4da6, 0 0 50px #ff4da6, 0 0 60px #ff4da6, 0 0 70px
#ff4da6, 0 0 80px #ff4da6;

  }

}


.shake:hover {

  animation: shake 0.5s;

  animation-iteration-count: infinite;

}


@keyframes shake {

  0% { transform: translate(1px, 1px) rotate(0deg); }

  10% { transform: translate(-1px, -2px) rotate(-1deg); }

  20% { transform: translate(-3px, 0px) rotate(1deg); }

  30% { transform: translate(3px, 2px) rotate(0deg); }
```

```
    40% { transform: translate(1px, -1px) rotate(1deg); }
    50% { transform: translate(-1px, 2px) rotate(-1deg); }
    60% { transform: translate(-3px, 1px) rotate(0deg); }
    70% { transform: translate(3px, 1px) rotate(-1deg); }
    80% { transform: translate(-1px, -1px) rotate(1deg); }
    90% { transform: translate(1px, 2px) rotate(0deg); }
    100% { transform: translate(1px, -2px) rotate(-1deg); }
}


#1 {

  width: 20px;

  height: 20px;

}


#2 {

  width: 20px;

  height: 20px;

}


#3 {

  width: 20px;

  height: 20px;

}


.img {
```

```css
  -webkit-animation: myfirst 5s linear 2s infinite
alternate; /* Safari 4.0 - 8.0 */

  animation: myfirst 5s linear 2s infinite alternate;

}


body {

  position: relative;

}
</style>

    </head>

    <body>

        <div class="wrapper">



        <header style="width: 100%;">

          <div class="logo">

          <br><br>

          <img class="shake" width="90" height="90"
src="images/open.png">

          <h1 class="glow" style="color: lightgreen;">ONLINE
SCHOOL LIBRARY</h1>

      </div>


      <?php

      if(isset($_SESSION['login_user']))

      {

          ?>
```

```php
    <nav>
        <ul>
            <li><a href="index.php">HOME</a></li>
            <li><a href="books.php">BOOKS</a></li>
            <li><a href="logout.php">LOGOUT</a></li>
        </ul>
    </nav>
    <?php
    }
    else
    {?>
<nav>

            <ul>
                <li><a href="index.php">HOME</a></li>
                <li><a href="books.php">BOOKS</a></li>
                <li><a href="student_login.php">STUDENT-
LOGIN</a></li>
            </ul>
        </nav>
    <?php
    }


    ?>
```

```
        </header>

        <section style="width: 100%">

                <div class="sec_img" style="position:
relative;">

                        <center><img class="shake img" width="200"
height="200" id="3" src="http://1.bp.blogspot.com/-
4YLS0VUehYA/Uj8c1HGuVII/AAAAAAAAMow/EdmSkoRrcmQ/s1600/kids
-sitting-on-books.png"></center>

                <br><br><br>

                <div class="box">

                        <br><br><br><br>

                                <h1 style="text-align: center; font-size:
35px;">Welcome to Online School Library</h1><br><br>

                </div>

                </div>

        </section>

        </div>


<br><br><br><br><br><br><br><br><br><br><br><br><br><b
r><br><br><br>

        <?php

        include "footer.php";

        ?>

        </body>

</html>
```

It looks like this:

Figure 7-12: index.php on student.php

This is the code for **student_login.php**:

```php
<?php

    include "connection.php";

    include "navbar.php";

?>


<!DOCTYPE html>

<html>

    <head>

        <title>

            Student Login

        </title>

        <link rel="stylesheet" href="css/style.css">

        <meta charset="utf-8">

        <meta name="viewport" content="width=device-width,
initial-scale=1">
```

140

```
        <style>
/*------------------------------Main Code   INDEX -------
-----------------------------------------------*/


.wrapper

{

    height: 100%;

    width: 100%;

    /*background-color: red;*/



}

header

{

        height: 130px;

        width: 1536px;

        background-color: black;

}

section

{

    height: 100%;

    width: 100%;

    background-color: white;

}

footer

{
```

```
        width: 1536px;

        background-color: black;

}

navbar {

  width: 100%;

}

.logo

{

        float: left;

        padding-left: 20px;



}

.logo img

{

        padding-left: 80px;

}


li a

{

   color: white;

   text-decoration: none;



}

/*nav

{

  float: right;
```

```css
    word-spacing: 30px;

    padding: 20px;

}

nav li

{

    display: inline-block;

    line-height: 80px;

}*/


section .sec_img

{

    height: 550px;

    margin-top: 0px;

    background-image: url("images/background.png");

}

.box

{

    height: 300px;

    width: 450px;

    background-color: green;

    margin: 70px auto;

    opacity: .8;

    color: blue;

}
/*-------------------------------student login-----------
-----------*/
```

```
.log_img
{
    height: 100%;
    width: 100%;
    margin-top: 0px;
    background-image: url("images/whitelibrary.jpg");
}
.box1
{
    height: 450px;
    width: 450px;
    background-color: green;
    margin: 70px auto;
    opacity: .8;
    color: white;
    padding: 20px;
}
form .login
{
    margin: auto 50px;
}
input
{
    height: 25px;
    width: 300px;
}
```

```css
/*---------------------------registration-------------
-------*/

.reg_img

{

    height: 630px;

    margin-top: 0px;

    background-image: url("images/background3.png");

}

.box2

{

    height: 589px;

    width: 490px;

    background-color: green;

    marqin: 0px auto;

    opacity: .8;

    color: white;

    padding: 20px;

}

form .Registration

{

    margin: auto 50px;

}

        </style>


<link rel="stylesheet"
href="https://maxcdn.bootstrapcdn.com/bootstrap/3.4.0/css/
bootstrap.min.css">
```

```
<script
src="https://ajax.googleapis.com/ajax/libs/jquery/3.4.0/jq
uery.min.js"></script>

<script
src="https://maxcdn.bootstrapcdn.com/bootstrap/3.4.0/js/bo
otstrap.min.js"></script>

    </head>

<body>

    <section style="height: 670px;">

        <div class="log_img">

                <br><br><br>

                <center><div class="box1">

                <br><br>

                    <h1 style="text-align: center; font-
size: 35px; font-family: Lucida Console;">Library
Management System</h1><br>

                    <h1 style="text-align: center; font-
size: 25px;">User Login Form</h1>

                    <form name="login" action=""
method="post">

                <div class="login">

                    <input class="form-control"
type="text" name="username" placeholder="Username"
required=""><br>

                    <input class="form-control"
type="password" name="password" placeholder="Password"
required=""><br>

                    <input class="btn btn-default"
type="submit" name="submit" value="Login" style="color:
#429619; width: 70px; height: 30px;"> </div></form>

                </div></center>

        </div>

    </section>
```

```php
<?php


    if(isset($_POST['submit']))

    {

        $count=0;

        $res=mysqli_query($db,"SELECT * FROM student WHERE
username='$_POST[username]' &&
password='$_POST[password]';");


        $row= mysqli_fetch_assoc($res);

        $count=mysqli_num_rows($res);


        if($count==0)

        {

        ?>

        <!--

        <script>

            alert("The username and password don't exist.")

        </script>

        -->

        <div class="alert alert-danger" style="width:
700px; margin-left: 360px; background-color: rgb(132, 57,
57); color: white; border-color:rgb(8, 23, 3, 10);">

            <strong>The username and password don't
exist.</strong>

        </div>

    <?php
```

```php
            }
        else{
            $_SESSION['login_user'] = $_POST['username'];
            $_SESSION['pic']= $row['pic'];


            ?>
            <script>
              window.location="index.php";
            </script>
              <?php
        }
        }


        ?>


</body>
</html>
```

This is how it looks:

Figure 7-12: How the student login looks

Here is the complete for **books.php**:

```php
<?php

    include "connection.php";

    include "navbar.php";


    $ms = "SELECT * FROM student WHERE
username='$_SESSION[login_user]'";
    $d = mysqli_query($db, $ms);
    $rows = mysqli_fetch_assoc($d);


    $first = $rows['first'];
    $last = $rows['last'];
    $name = "Welcome, ".$first." ".$last;
?>
<!DOCTYPE HTML>
<html>
```

```html
    <head>

        <title>Books</title>

        <meta name="viewport" content="width=device-width,
initial-scale=1">


        <style>

            .srch

            {

                padding-left: 1000px;

            }


              * {box-sizing: border-box;}
body {font-family: Verdana, sans-serif;}
.mySlides {display: none;}
img {vertical-align: middle;}


/* Slideshow container */
.slideshow-container {
  max-width: 1000px;
  position: relative;
  margin: auto;
}


/* Caption text */
.text {
  color: #f2f2f2;
```

```css
    font-size: 15px;

    padding: 8px 12px;

    position: absolute;

    bottom: 8px;

    width: 100%;

    text-align: center;
}


/* Number text (1/3 etc) */
.numbertext {

    color: #f2f2f2;

    font-size: 12px;

    padding: 8px 12px;

    position: absolute;

    top: 0;
}


/* The dots/bullets/indicators */
.dot {

    height: 15px;

    width: 15px;

    margin: 0 2px;

    background-color: #bbb;

    border-radius: 50%;

    display: inline-block;

    transition: background-color 0.6s ease;
```

```css
}

.active {
  background-color: #717171;
}

/* Fading animation */
.fade {
  -webkit-animation-name: fade;
  -webkit-animation-duration: 1.5s;
  animation-name: fade;
  animation-duration: 1.5s;
}

@-webkit-keyframes fade {
  from {opacity: .4}
  to {opacity: 1}
}

@keyframes fade {
  from {opacity: .4}
  to {opacity: 1}
}

/* On smaller screens, decrease text size */
@media only screen and (max-width: 300px) {
```

```css
    .text {font-size: 11px}
}


body {
    font-family: "Lato", sans-serif;
    transition: background-color .5s;
    margin-right: 100px;
}


.sidenav {
    height: 100%;
    margin-top: 50px;
    width: 0;
    position: fixed;
    z-index: 1;
    top: 0;
    left: 0;
    background-color: lightgreen;
    overflow-x: hidden;
    transition: 0.5s;
    padding-top: 60px;
}


.sidenav a {
    padding: 8px 8px 8px 32px;
```

```css
    text-decoration: none;

    font-size: 25px;

    color: #818181;

    display: block;

    transition: 0.3s;

}


.sidenav a:hover {

    color: #f1f1f1;

}


.sidenav .closebtn {

    position: absolute;

    top: 0;

    right: 25px;

    font-size: 36px;

    margin-left: 50px;

}


#main {

    transition: margin-left .5s;

    padding: 16px;

}


@media screen and (max-height: 450px) {

    .sidenav {padding-top: 15px;}
```

```css
    .sidenav a {font-size: 18px;}

}


.img-circle

{

    margin-left: 20px;

}


.pop:hover

{

    color: white;

    width: 300px;

    height: 50px;

    background-color: blue;

}


    </style>
```

```html
<link rel="stylesheet"
href="https://maxcdn.bootstrapcdn.com/bootstrap/3.4.0/css/
bootstrap.min.css">

<script
src="https://ajax.googleapis.com/ajax/libs/jquery/3.4.0/jq
uery.min.js"></script>

<script
src="https://maxcdn.bootstrapcdn.com/bootstrap/3.4.0/js/bo
otstrap.min.js"></script>

    </head>

    <body>
```

```
        <!--
_____sidenav_____
_____-->


    <div id="mySidenav" class="sidenav" style="text-
decoration: none;">

  <a href="javascript:void(0)" class="closebtn"
onclick="closeNav()" style="text-decoration:
none;">&times;</a>



                    <div style="color: white; margin-
left: 60px; font-size: 20px;">

                    <?php

                    if(isset($_SESSION['login_user']))

                        { echo "<img class='img-circle
profile_img' height=120 width=120
src='images/".$_SESSION['pic']."'>";

                    echo "</br></br>";



                    echo $name;

                    }

                    ?>

                    </div><br><br>


<div class="pop">  <a href="issue_info.php" style="text-
decoration: none;">Issue Information</a> </div>

</div>


<div id="main">

  <span style="font-size:30px;cursor:pointer"
onclick="openNav()">&#9776; open</span>
```

```
<script>

function openNav() {

  document.getElementById("mySidenav").style.width =
"300px";

  document.getElementById("main").style.marginLeft =
"300px";

  document.body.style.backgroundColor = "rgba(0,0,0,0.4)";

}


function closeNav() {

  document.getElementById("mySidenav").style.width = "0";

  document.getElementById("main").style.marginLeft= "0";

  document.body.style.backgroundColor = "white";

}

</script>

     <!--_____search
bar_____-->


     <div class="srch">

        <form class="navbar-form" method="POST"
name="form1">

              <input class="form-control" type="text"
name="search" placeholder="Search for a book..."
required="">

              <button style="background-color:
lightgreen;" type="submit" name="search" class="btn btn-
default">
```

```
                        <span class="glyphicon glyphicon-
search"></span>

                </button><br><br>

        </form>

        <form method="POST" class="navbar-form"
name="form2">

                        <input class="form-control"
type="text" name="bid" placeholder="Search for a Book
ID..." required="">

                        <button style="background-color:
lightgreen;" type="submit" name="reserve" class="btn btn-
default">Reserve a Book</button><br>

        </form>

</div>

        <?php

        if(isset($_POST['search']))

        {

            include "search.php";

            $books = "SELECT * FROM books WHERE title
LIKE'%$_POST[search]%'";

    $run = mysqli_query($db, $books);

    $rows = mysqli_fetch_array($run);


    $bid = $rows['bid'];

    $isbn = $rows['isbn'];

    $btitle = $rows['title'];

    $bauthor = $rows['authors'];

    $bpublisher = $rows['publisher'];

    $quantity = $rows['quantity'];
```

```php
$bsection = $rows['section'];

$description = $rows['description'];

$bimage = $rows['image'];

    if(mysqli_num_rows($q)==0)

    {

        echo "Sorry, I didn't get that. Try
checking: <br> 1. Spelling <br> 2. Try another phrase <br>
3. The book does not exist";

    }

    else

    {

        echo "<table class='table table-bordered
table-hover'>";

        // Table rows(tr)

        echo "<tr style='background-color:
lightgreen;'>";

        // Table header(th)

        echo "<th>";  echo "ID";        echo "</th>";

        echo "<th>";  echo "ISBN No.";  echo "</th>";

        echo "<th>";  echo "Title";     echo "</th>";

        echo "<th>";  echo "Author(s)"; echo "</th>";

        echo "<th>";  echo "Publisher"; echo "</th>";

        echo "<th>";  echo "Status";    echo "</th>";

        echo "<th>";  echo "Quantity";  echo "</th>";

        echo "<th>";  echo "Section";   echo "</th>";


        echo "</tr>";
```

```php
while($row=mysqli_fetch_array($q))

{

echo "<tr>";

// Table data(td)

    echo "<td>"; echo $row['bid']; echo "</td>";

    echo "<td>"; echo $row['isbn']; echo "</td>";

    echo "<td><button id='open' class='btn btn-
info'>Preview</button>    "; echo $row['title'];
echo "</a></td>";

    echo "<td>"; echo $row['authors']; echo "</td>";

    echo "<td>"; echo $row['publisher']; echo "</td>";

    echo "<td>"; echo $row['status']; echo "</td>";

    echo "<td>"; echo $row['quantity']; echo "</td>";

    echo "<td>"; echo $row['section']; echo "</td>";


    echo "</tr>";

}

    echo "</table>";

        }

            echo "<!-- The Modal -->
<div id='myModal' class='modal'>


  <!-- Modal content -->

  <center><div class='modal-content' style='width:
500px;'>

    <div style='background-color: lightgreen;'
class='modal-header'>
```

```html
        <span style='color: black; background-color: grey;
padding-left: 3px; padding-right: 3px; padding-bottom:
3px; padding-top: 3px;' class='close'>&times;</span>

        <h2>$btitle</h2>

    </div>

    <div class='modal-body'>

        <img src='$bimage' width=210 height=300 alt='$btitle
cover' style='float: right;'>

        <p>$description</p>

        <p>Book ID: $bid</p>

        <p>ISBN No.: $isbn</p>

        <p>Section: $bsection</p>

        <p>Quantity: $quantity</p>

        <p>Publisher: $bpublisher</p>

    <div class='modal-footer'>

        <h3>By $bauthor</h3>

    </div>

  </div></center>


</div>

<script>
// Get the modal

var modal = document.getElementById('myModal');


// Get the button that opens the modal

var btn = document.getElementById('open');
```

```javascript
// Get the <span> element that closes the modal
var span = document.getElementsByClassName('close')[0];


// When the user clicks the button, open the modal
btn.onclick = function() {
  modal.style.display = 'block';
}


// When the user clicks on <span> (x), close the modal
span.onclick = function() {
  modal.style.display = 'none';
}


// When the user clicks anywhere outside of the modal,
close it
window.onclick = function(event) {
  if (event.target == modal) {
    modal.style.display = 'none';
  }
}
</script>
";
        }
            /* if button is not pressed */
          else {
          ?>
```

```
<center><div class="slideshow-container">


    <h1>Favourite Books</h1><br>


<div class="mySlides fade">

   <div class="numbertext">1 / 3</div>

   <img
src="http://cdn.shopify.com/s/files/1/0028/5468/2689/produ
cts/STIM9781407106175_BK_grande.jpg?v=1530118311"
style="width: 200px; height: 200px;">

   <br><br><br>

   <div class="text" style="color: blue;">Stick Man, Julia
Donaldson &amp; Axel Scheffler, 21 August 2008</div>

</div>


<div class="mySlides fade">

   <div class="numbertext">2 / 3</div>

   <img src="https://images-na.ssl-images-
amazon.com/images/I/51%2BV5g3Q9WL._SX324_BO1,204,203,200_.
jpg" style="width: 200px; height: 200px;">

   <br><br><br>

   <div class="text" style="color: blue;">Catching Falling
Stars, Karen McCombie, 4 June 2015</div>

</div>


<div class="mySlides fade">

   <div class="numbertext">3 / 3</div>
```

```
    <img src="https://images-na.ssl-images-
amazon.com/images/I/61t3K7PGljL._SX258_BO1,204,203,200_.jp
g" style="width: 200px; height: 200px;">

    <br><br><br>

    <div class="text" style="color: blue;">Farmer Duck,
Marin Waddell &amp; Helen Oxenbury, 1991</div>

</div>


</div> </center>

<br>


<div style="text-align:center">

    <span class="dot"></span>

    <span class="dot"></span>

    <span class="dot"></span>

</div>


<script>

var slideIndex = 0;

showSlides();


function showSlides() {

    var i;

    var slides =
document.getElementsByClassName("mySlides");

    var dots = document.getElementsByClassName("dot");

    for (i = 0; i < slides.length; i++) {

        slides[i].style.display = "none";
```

```
    }

    slideIndex++;

    if (slideIndex > slides.length) {slideIndex = 1}

    for (i = 0; i < dots.length; i++) {

        dots[i].className = dots[i].className.replace("
    active", "");

    }

    slides[slideIndex-1].style.display = "block";

    dots[slideIndex-1].className += " active";

    setTimeout(showSlides, 2000); // Change image every 2
    seconds

}

</script>


    <?php

    }

    if(isset($_SESSION['login_user'])) {

        if(isset($_POST['reserve'])) {

            $query = "INSERT INTO issue_book VALUES('',
    '$_SESSION[login_user]', '$_POST[bid]', 'Borrowed', NOW(),
    NOW() + INTERVAL 35 DAY)";

            $quant = "UPDATE books SET status='Not
    Available', quantity=quantity-1 WHERE
    books.bid=$_POST[bid]";

            $run = mysqli_query($db, $query);

            $run2 = mysqli_query($db, $quant);

        }

    }

        if(!isset($_SESSION['login_user']))
```

```php
            {
                ?>
                <script>
                    alert("Please login!");
                </script>
                <?php
            }


        ?>
    </body>
</html>
```

It looks like this:

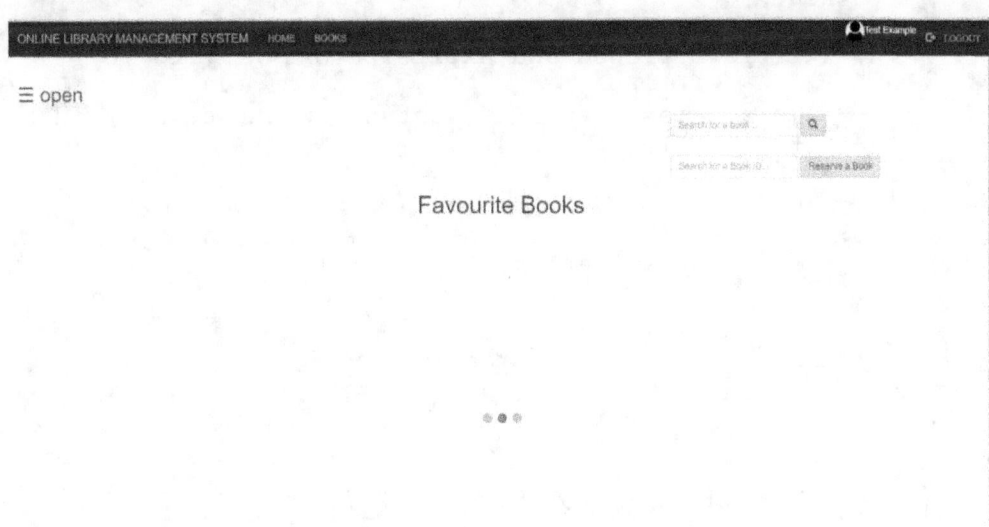

Figure 7-13: This is how books.php looks

Here is the code for ***issue_book.php***:

```php
<?php
    include "connection.php";
    include "navbar.php";
```

```php
$ms = "SELECT * FROM student WHERE
username='$_SESSION[login_user]'";

$d = mysqli_query($db, $ms);

$rows = mysqli_fetch_assoc($d);


$first = $rows['first'];

$last = $rows['last'];

$name = "Welcome, ".$first." ".$last;
?>
```

```html
<!DOCTYPE html>

<html>

<head>

  <title>Borrowed and Expired Books</title>

  <meta name="viewport" content="width=device-width,
initial-scale=1">


  <style type="text/css">


    .srch

    {

      padding-left: 850px;


    }

    .form-control

    {

      width: 300px;
```

```css
    height: 40px;

    background-color: white;

    color: black;

  }


  body {

    background-image: url("images/books.jpg");

    background-repeat: no-repeat;

    font-family: "Lato", sans-serif;

    transition: background-color .5s;

}


.sidenav {

  height: 100%;

  margin-top: 50px;

  width: 0;

  position: fixed;

  z-index: 1;

  top: 0;

  left: 0;

  background-color: lightgreen;

  overflow-x: hidden;

  transition: 0.5s;

  padding-top: 60px;

}
```

```css
.sidenav a {
  padding: 8px 8px 8px 32px;
  text-decoration: none;
  font-size: 25px;
  color: #818181;
  display: block;
  transition: 0.3s;
}


.sidenav a:hover {
  color: white;
}


.sidenav .closebtn {
  position: absolute;
  top: 0;
  right: 25px;
  font-size: 36px;
  margin-left: 50px;
}

#main {
  transition: margin-left .5s;
  padding: 16px;
}
```

```css
@media screen and (max-height: 450px) {
  .sidenav {padding-top: 15px;}
  .sidenav a {font-size: 18px;}
}
.img-circle
{
  margin-left: 20px;
}
.h:hover
{
  color: white;
  width: 300px;
  height: 50px;
  background-color: blue;
}
.container
{
  height: 600px;
  background-color: white;
  opacity: .8;
  color: black;
}
.scroll
{
  width: 100%;
  height: 500px;
```

```
    overflow: auto;

}

th,td

{

  width: 10%;

}


  </style>


</head>

<body>

<!--_____sidenav_____-->


  <div id="mySidenav" class="sidenav">

  <a href="javascript:void(0)" class="closebtn"
onclick="closeNav()">&times;</a>


      <div style="color: white; margin-left: 60px; font-
size: 20px;">


           <?php

           if(isset($_SESSION['login_user']))


               {   echo "<img class='img-circle
profile_img' height=120 width=120
src='images/".$_SESSION['pic']."'>";

               echo "</br></br>";
```

```
                    echo $name;

                }

                ?>

        </div><br><br>


    <div class="h"> <a href="books.php">Books</a></div>

    <div class="h"> <a href="issue_info.php">Issue
Information</a></div>

</div>


<div id="main">


    <span style="font-size:30px;cursor:pointer"
onclick="openNav()">&#9776; open</span>



    <script>

    function openNav() {

        document.getElementById("mySidenav").style.width =
"300px";

        document.getElementById("main").style.marginLeft =
"300px";

        document.body.style.backgroundColor =
"rgba(0,0,0,0.4)";

    }


    function closeNav() {
```

```php
        document.getElementById("mySidenav").style.width =
"0";

        document.getElementById("main").style.marginLeft= "0";

        document.body.style.backgroundColor = "white";

    }

    </script>

    <div class="container">

        <h3 style="text-align: center;">Borrowed and Expired
Books</h3><br>

        <?php

        $c=0;


            if(isset($_SESSION['login_user']))

            {

            $exp = "<p style='color: yellow; background-color:
red;'>EXPIRED</p>";

            $ret = "<p style='color: yellow; background-color:
green;'>RETURNED</p>";

            $sql="SELECT
student.username,id,books.bid,title,authors,publisher,appr
ove,borrow_date,return_date FROM student inner join
issue_book ON student.username=issue_book.username inner
join books ON issue_book.bid=books.bid WHERE
issue_book.username ='$_SESSION[login_user]' AND
issue_book.approve !='' ORDER BY
`issue_book`.`return_date` ASC";

            $res=mysqli_query($db,$sql);


            echo "<table class='table table-bordered'
style='width:100%;' >";

            //Table header
```

```php
        echo "<tr style='background-color: lightgreen;'>";

        echo "<th>"; echo "Book ID";  echo "</th>";

        echo "<th>"; echo "Book Title";  echo "</th>";

        echo "<th>"; echo "Authors";  echo "</th>";

        echo "<th>"; echo "Publisher";  echo "</th>";

        echo "<th>"; echo "Status"; echo "</th>";

        echo "<th>"; echo "Issue Date";  echo "</th>";

        echo "<th>"; echo "Return Date";  echo "</th>";


    echo "</tr>";
    echo "</table>";


  echo "<div class='scroll'>";
    echo "<table class='table table-bordered' >";
while($row=mysqli_fetch_assoc($res))
    {


    echo "<tr>";
        echo "<td>"; echo $row['bid']; echo "</td>";

        echo "<td>"; echo $row['title']; echo "</td>";

        echo "<td>"; echo $row['authors']; echo "</td>";

        echo "<td>"; echo $row['publisher']; echo
"</td>";

        echo "<td>"; echo $row['approve']; echo "</td>";

        echo "<td>"; echo $row['borrow_date']; echo
"</td>";
```

```php
            echo "<td>"; echo $row['return_date']; echo
"</td>";

        echo "</tr>";

        }

    echo "</table>";

        echo "</div>";



        }

        else

        {

        ?>

            <h4 style="text-align: center;">Please
Login</h4>

        <?php

        }

    ?>
    </div>
</div>
</body>
</html>
```

It looks like this:

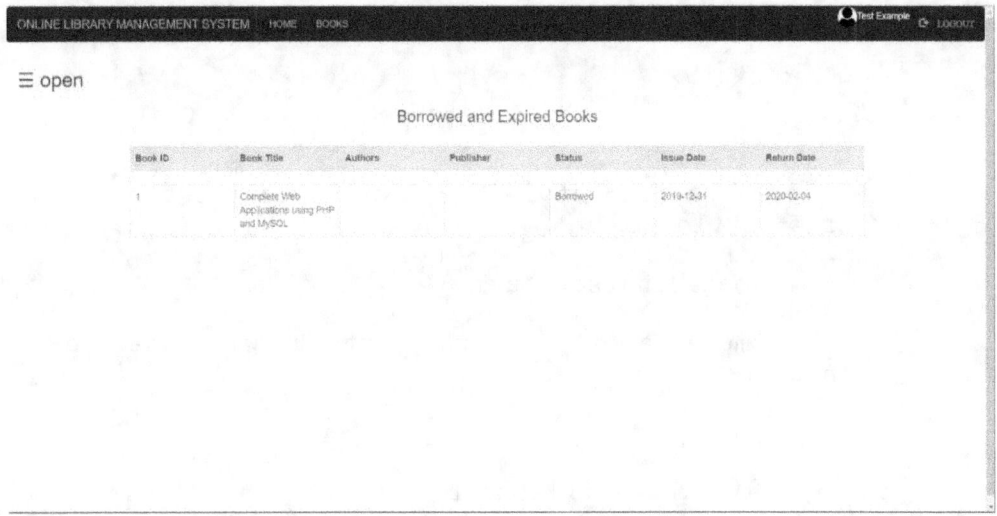

Figure 7-14: How issue_book.php looks

This is the code for **navbar.php**:

```php
<?php
  session_start();


  $user = $_SESSION['login_user'];
  $get_user = "SELECT * FROM student WHERE
username='$user'";
  $run_user = mysqli_query($db, $get_user);
  $row = mysqli_fetch_array($run_user);


  $first = $row['first'];
  $last = $row['last'];
?>
<!DOCTYPE html>
<html>
<head>
```

```html
<title>

</title>



    <link rel="stylesheet" type="text/css"
href="style.css">

    <meta charset="utf-8">

    <meta name="viewport" content="width=device-width,
initial-scale=1">



    <link rel="stylesheet"
href="https://maxcdn.bootstrapcdn.com/bootstrap/3.3.7/css/
bootstrap.min.css">

    <script
src="https://ajax.googleapis.com/ajax/libs/jquery/3.3.1/jq
uery.min.js"></script>

    <script
src="https://maxcdn.bootstrapcdn.com/bootstrap/3.3.7/js/bo
otstrap.min.js"></script>



</head>

<body>



        <nav class="navbar navbar-inverse">

    <div class="container-fluid">

        <div class="navbar-header">

            <a class="navbar-brand active"
style="background-color: #222;">ONLINE LIBRARY MANAGEMENT
SYSTEM</a>

        </div>

        <ul class="nav navbar-nav">

            <li><a href="index.php">HOME</a></li>
```

```php
        <li><a href="books.php">BOOKS</a></li>

    </ul>

    <?php

        if(isset($_SESSION['login_user']))

        {?>

            <ul class="nav navbar-nav">

                        <!-- <li><a
href="profile.php">PROFILE</a></li> -->

                </ul>


            <ul class="nav navbar-nav navbar-right">

                <li>

                    <div style="color: white">


                    <?php

                        echo "<img class='img-circle
profile_img' height=30 width=30
src='images/".$_SESSION['pic']."'>";

                        echo "$first $last";

                    ?>

                </div></li>

                <li><a href="logout.php"><span
class="glyphicon glyphicon-log-out">
LOGOUT</span></a></li>


            </ul>

        <?php

        }
```

```php
            else

            {     ?>

                <ul class="nav navbar-nav navbar-right">


                    <li><a href="student_login.php"><span
class="glyphicon glyphicon-log-in"> LOGIN</span></a></li>


                </ul>

                <?php

            }

        ?>




        </div>

    </nav>

</body>

</html>
```

This is the complete code for *footer.php*:

```php
<!DOCTYPE html>

<html>

    <head>

        <title></title>


        <meta charset="utf-8">

        <meta name="viewport" content="width=device-width,
initial-scale=1">
```

```
<link rel="stylesheet"
href="https://cdnjs.cloudflare.com/ajax/libs/font-
awesome/4.7.0/css/font-awesome.min.css">


<style>


footer

{

  height: 100px;

  width: 100%;

  background-color: black;

}


  .fa

  {

    margin: 0px 5px;

    padding: 5px;

    font-size: 20px;

    width: 20px;

    height: 20px;

    text-align: center;

    text-decoration: none;

    border-radius: 50%;

  }


  .fa:hover

  {
```

```css
    opacity: .7;

}


.fa-facebook

{

    background-color: #3B5998;

    color: white;

}


.fa-twitter

{

    background-color: #55ACEE;

    color: white;

}


.fa-google

{

    background-color: #dd4b39;

    color: white;

}


.fa-instagram

{

    background-color: #125688;

    color: white;

}
```

```
        .fa-yahoo

        {

            background-color: #400297;

            color: white;

        }


    </style>


    </head>

    <body>

        <footer style="background-color: black; width:
100%;">

        <br>

        <h3 style="color: white; text-align:
center;"><em>Email:  example@example.com</em>
<strong>Contact Us through social media.</strong>
<i>Contact:  01234567891</i></h3><br>


        <div style="">


        <center><a href="#" class="fa fa-facebook"></a>

        <a href="#" class="fa fa-twitter"></a>

        <a href="#" class="fa fa-google"></a>

        <a href="#" class="fa fa-instagram"></a>

        <a href="#" class="fa fa-yahoo"></a></center>

    </div>

        </footer>
```

```
    </body>
</html>
```

This is how it looks:

Figure 7-15: How footer.php looks

This is the complete code for **search.php**:

```php
<?php

$search_query = $_POST['search'];

    $q=mysqli_query($db,"SELECT * FROM books WHERE title
LIKE'%$_POST[search]%'");

    $books = "SELECT * FROM books WHERE title
LIKE'%$_POST[search]%'";

    $run = mysqli_query($db, $books);

    $rows = mysqli_fetch_array($run);

?>
```

Finally, here is the code for **logout.php**:

```php
<?php

    session_start();

    if(isset($_SESSION['login_user']))

    {

        unset($_SESSION['login_user']);

    }

    header("location:index.php");

?>
```

Well done! You have completed the project! I hope you have learned something new.

About the Author

Rumaysa Ahmed is a young author. She started coding when she was five and has been coding ever since. Rumaysa will love to see all young children alike to be able to code. Rumaysa has built many websites, attended various coding events including hackathons. She also enjoys mathematics, baking and fashion designing. Rumaysa is also writing fiction stories.

www.ingramcontent.com/pod-product-compliance
Lightning Source LLC
Chambersburg PA
CBHW080009210526
45170CB00015B/1950